To Rev. James O Gay +
Mrs. Gay

From
Clayton +
4 - 1 - 79

FOR SUCH A TIME AS THIS

For Such a Time as This

Harold L. Rice

Exposition Press   *Hicksville, New York*

All Scripture printed herein is taken from the King James Version of the Bible, unless otherwise noted.

FIRST EDITION

© 1976 by Harold L. Rice

ISBN 0-682-48618-3

Printed in the United States of America

Dedication

This book is dedicated to my family, who, while it was in preparation, were denied the many hours of enjoyment of husband and father, as was their due.

Also, I dedicate this book to my many instructors in the Word, especially to my parents, whose early guidance to me in the Word has a great bearing on the contents of the book.

And I dedicate this book to Mrs. Charlotte Hardin, whose faithful work in correction, typing and manuscripting has been an invaluable aid in the completion of it. Without that which she has supplied, it would not have been completed.

Contents

I

The Seventy Weeks of the Prophecy of Daniel

Though there are many sermons preached on this subject, I have found in my work and in talking with people that there are very few Bible lessons where the truth can be learned. We are seeking the truth, without bias, concerning this subject.

In the study of prophecy, particularly of the second coming of Christ, certain things must be understood and kept in mind. God deals with three groups of people in the Bible concerning His purposes for the world and the Age of Man. The first group is the Gentile nations; the second is the nation of Israel; and the third is the Church.

In speaking of the Church, one must understand that simply to have one's name recorded on a church roster does not constitute membership in the true Church, the Bride of Christ. This comes from within, in born-again believers and followers of Christ, no matter what denomination, color or nationality. The Church to which we refer is made up of people who believe in and follow Christ.

To interpret Scripture properly it is necessary to know which group is involved in the context of the Word. For instance, if God is speaking to the Gentiles, and you apply it to the Jews, the entire line of prophetic fulfillment of the Scripture is disrupted. It is the same with any Scripture that is spoken to the Jew, or to the Church, if we apply it to the other group.

This is the reason for so many varied interpretations of prophetic events. They clash with each other and lead to frustration in the study of prophecy. The Bible test of the veracity of a prophet is simply this: Did his prophecies come true? We would be confused about whether some prophecies came true or not unless we recognize that in some instances God is speaking to the Gentile world, in others He speaks to the nation of Israel, and in others to the Church. We must learn to properly apply the context of the Scripture we are studying. It is very important that we keep these three groups and the prophecies that relate to them separated.

In the first pages of this study we shall examine the prophecy of God in dealing with the Jews as a nation. This prophecy is outlined in a period of seventy weeks of years. (We shall discuss these "weeks of years" more fully later in this chapter.)

Much of the fulfillment of Daniel's prophecy hinges upon an event in 1948—Israel became a nation. All the events of the twenty-fourth and twenty-fifth chapters of the book of Matthew, and Christ's returning soon, also hinge upon this event.

There have been six great world empires that have tried to destroy God's people on earth, Israel. In studying the Scriptures we learn that after God called Abraham out into the land of promise, He told him that through his seed all the nations would be blessed.

Abraham begat Isaac, and Isaac begat Esau and Jacob. Jacob, through deceit, obtained the blessing from Isaac, and in the course of time had twelve sons. In Genesis 35:10 we read, "And God said unto him, Thy name is Jacob: thy name shall not be called any more Jacob, but Israel shall be thy name: and he called his name Israel." The twelve sons of Israel eventually became the heads of the twelve tribes of Israel, the nation.

While still a family under the same roof, Israel and his sons were forced to go to live in Egypt due to a great famine in their own land. They remained there for four hundred years. The Egyptians tried to destroy the Israelites, or make them ineffective as a nation, by forcing them into slavery and bondage.

It has been the business of Satan, from the beginning of time, to destroy the seed of the woman through whom the Redeemer would come as God promised in the Garden of Eden (Genesis 3:15). Mary, the mother of Jesus, was a descendant of Abraham. Therefore, Egypt became the first great power who tried to destroy the witness of Israel to the One True God from the face of the earth.

After the Israelites had fled from the rule of the Egyptian Empire with the help of God and regained their identity in their own land, the Assyrian empire took away their freedom. It is noted in the Old Testament that the Assyrians were a race of people that became strong suddenly. They were initially a weak nation, but God strengthened them and raised them up to punish His people because they were disobedient to His revealed will and command. Assyria became a mighty nation that harassed and tore asunder the people of God, but they could not destroy the Jewish people who are God's witness on earth.

After the Assyrian Empire came the Babylonian Empire. This was the third great world power to try, through the influence of Satan, to destroy the Israelite people and prevent the Redeemer from coming to save men. The Israelites were taken into Babylon in captivity and spent many years there in slavery and bondage. The record of their captivity is an important part of Jewish history.

The Jewish people were eventually allowed their freedom once more, and they again established themselves as a nation in their homeland. Once more they were conquered, this time by the Persian Empire. The record of Belshazzar, one of its great rulers, is found in the book of Daniel. We read of his wickedness and the hand of God writing on the wall to warn Belshazzar of his doom.

Darius, the Mede, ruled Persia during Israel's captivity, and was greatly influenced by God's prophet, Daniel. This is also recorded in the book of Daniel.

The Persian Empire was followed in power over the Israelites by the Grecian Empire. This becomes important to us now because at the end of the Age of the Gentiles, in which we are now living, a form of the Grecian Empire will be revived. The antichrist will come from the part of the world this empire embraces. The Scriptures predict that the antichrist will come from Syria, a relatively small nation. He will surprise the nations because he comes from such obscurity and assumes such great power.

The empire of Greece gave way to the great iron kingdom of Rome. This was the sixth world power to hold dominion over the Jewish people. Rome ruled the world when Jesus was born. Daniel prophesied in the ninth chapter of his book of Jesus' birth and crucifixion. This is known by Bible commentators the world over as the sixty-ninth week of the prophecy of Daniel.

Now let us examine particularly the twenty-fourth verse of that ninth chapter of the book of Daniel:

> Seventy weeks are determined upon thy people and upon thy holy city, to finish the transgression, and to make an end of sins, and to make reconciliation for iniquity, and to bring in everlasting righteousness, and to seal up the vision and prophecy, and to anoint the most Holy.

It is important that we know about these weeks and recognize them as weeks of years when God is dealing only with the nation of Israel. By "weeks of years" we are referring to a period of seven years as being one week of years, just as seven days make up one week. Therefore the seventy weeks of Daniel's prophecy are actually 490 years.

Here again we must clarify to whom God is speaking in this particular prophecy. This is a prophecy concerning the Israelite nation. "Seventy weeks are determined upon *thy people* and upon thy holy city." Who are Daniel's people? They are the Jews. Which city is the "holy city" of the Jews? It is Jerusalem. Seventy weeks are determined upon the Jews and upon Jerusalem.

In Daniel 9:25-27 Daniel says:

Know therefore and understand, that from the going forth of the commandment to restore and to build Jerusalem unto the Messiah the Prince shall be seven weeks, and threescore and two weeks: the street shall be built again, and the wall, even in troublous times.

And after threescore and two weeks shall Messiah be cut off, but not for himself: and the people of the prince that shall come shall destroy the city and the sanctuary; and the end thereof shall be with a flood, and unto the end of the war desolations are determined.

And he shall confirm the covenant with many for one week: and in the midst of the week he shall cause the sacrifice and the oblation to cease, and for the overspreading of abominations he shall make it desolate, even until the consummation, and that determined shall be poured upon the desolate.

Seven weeks, threescore and two weeks add up to sixty-nine weeks of years. Daniel says that certain events will transpire at this time. We know that Daniel is speaking of seventy weeks of years because in the context is his prayer to God concerning some events of years. God sent an angel to answer Daniel's prayer, and the answer is given as an answer of years. The Hebrew word used here in the original language means literally seventy weeks of years. This totals 490 years.

We may know this is a week of years by examining the last week, the last seven days, as evidence. In other parts of the Bible where this specific time is spoken of, it is referred to as a period of seven years. This is Biblical proof that the seventy weeks of prophecy to be visited upon the people of Israel is seventy weeks of years.

As you will note in reading further, these weeks of years are not consecutive. After the first seven weeks (forty-nine years) comes a division. Following this interlude comes threescore and two weeks (434 years). Here there is another division. Then comes the last week (seven years).

The first forty-nine years was for the rebuilding of Jerusalem after it had been destroyed by the Babylonians. This prophecy was given to Daniel while the Israelites were still in captivity. Nehemiah was allowed to return to Jerusalem and rebuild the wall of the city. Forty-nine years after the third decree of King Artexerxes, the temple was rebuilt. This completed the first seven weeks of prophecy.

The second division, which totals 434 years, extends from the time the temple was completed until Jesus was crucified. The last period of time in Daniel's prophecy concerns the last seven years of this age. We do not know when this period will begin. Many believe that since Israel is once again established as a nation in her own land, according to prophecy and the signs of the times, we are now in the preliminary time of this period. Many believe that we will soon see God fulfilling this prophecy of Daniel concerning the Israelite nation.

The Gospel Age must come to an end. We believe that we are living in that time period because of the fact that Israel is established as a nation once more. Just as the prophecy states that Israel will be a troublesome plague to the nations, Israel is today a heartbreaking sore point to the world.

Though they are under fire from many areas, the people of Israel enjoy relative peace and freedom, as compared to their hundreds of years of captivity, displacement and bondage. However, this will soon come to an end as events begin to unfold that are foretold.

The entire 490 years to be fulfilled concerning the nation of Israel have been outlined. Needless to say, while these years are being fulfilled, the rest of the world will experience some of the problems that accompany the fulfillment.

By examining the Scriptures we learn that the Church does not experience the period called the "tribulation." The Church has the promise of deliverance from the wrath of God to come.

> For God hath not appointed us to wrath, but to obtain salvation by our Lord Jesus Christ. (I Thessalonians 5:9)

The Lord has promised to descend from heaven with a shout and to "out-resurrect" the righteous dead and to snatch away (the Greek word is *harpazo*) the righteous living. These righteous souls will proceed with Him to the Judgment Seat of Christ, which is solely for the judging of the saints.

At no time during the scattering of the Jews among the nations have any of the years of this prophecy been fulfilled. The years during their captivity in Babylon were unnumbered. With the rebuilding of the temple during Nehemiah's reign, the fulfillment resumed.

At the time when Jesus was born, the nation of Israel was under the sponsorship of Rome. Still, Israel was recognized as a separate state, a distinguished class of people. With Jesus' death the first 483 years of this prophecy came to an end.

From A.D. 70 to A.D. 1948 the Israelites have been scattered to the uttermost parts of the earth. Today there are millions of Jews in Palestine, and there are more returning to their homeland daily.

The flag of the nation of Israel flies in most of the embassies of the world, and it is once more time for God to begin dealing with them. The fulfillment of this last seven years of prophecy concerning Daniel's people will soon come to pass.

Certain things will transpire during this end time. First of all, the angel said to Daniel, "These [seven years of trouble, or the tribulation period] will be to put an end to transgression." The word *transgression* means rebellious activity against lawful authority. This has reference to the sins of the Jewish nation. This nation has sinned grievously since its inception from idol worship to rejection of Jesus Christ as Messiah. These sins will not end until the appearance to the earth of the Messiah, at the end of the seven-year tribulation period. The apostle Paul wrote concerning this in his letter to the Christians in Rome, as recorded in Romans 11:25-29:

> For I would not, brethren, that ye should be ignorant of this mystery, lest ye should be wise in your own conceits; that blindness in part is happened to Israel, until the fulness of the Gentiles be come in.
>
> And so all Israel shall be saved: as it is written, there shall

come out of Sion the Deliverer, and shall turn away ungodliness from Jacob:

For this is my covenant unto them, when I shall take away their sins.

As concerning the gospel, they are enemies for your sakes: but as touching the election, they are beloved for the fathers' sakes.

For the gifts and calling of God are without repentance.

In the Old Testament, the Prophet Isaiah spoke of this time.

Before she travailed, she brought forth; before her pain came, she was delivered of a man child.

Who hath heard such a thing? who hath seen such things? Shall the earth be made to bring forth in one day? or shall a nation be born at once? for as soon as Zion travailed, she brought forth her children.

Shall I bring to the birth, and not cause to bring forth? saith the Lord: shall I cause to bring forth, and shut the womb? saith thy God?

Rejoice ye with Jerusalem, and be glad with her, all ye that love her: rejoice for joy with her, all ye that mourn for her. (Isaiah 66:7-10)

Again, Ezekiel was inspired to write of this time in the book of Ezekiel, chapter 36, verses 24-30:

For I will take you from among the heathen and gather you out of all countries, and will bring you into your own land.

Then will I sprinkle clean water upon you, and ye shall be clean: from all your filthiness, and from all your idols, will I cleanse you.

A new heart also will I give you, and a new spirit will I put within you: and I will take away the stony heart out of your flesh, and I will give you an heart of flesh.

And I will put my spirit within you, and cause you to walk in my statutes, and ye shall keep my judgments, and do them.

And ye shall dwell in the land that I gave to your fathers; and ye shall be my people, and I will be your God. I will also save you from all your uncleannesses: and I will call for the corn, and will increase it, and lay no famine upon you.

And I will multiply the fruit of the tree, and the increase of the field, that ye shall receive no more reproach of famine among the heathen.

Many Christians misunderstand the eleventh chapter of Romans because of its context. This chapter teaches that God is going to do a special work for the Jewish people, and who are we to question God's plan? In the New Testament Paul speaks of the time when the age of the Gentiles will be finished. He says that God will be reminded of His gifts and callings to the Jews, and He will restore them in the Way, bringing to them a new covenant.

There was objection by the established religionists of His day when Jesus came the first time, and again on Pentecost when, by the presence of the Holy Spirit, the Church Age began. The apostles had to deal with the resistance of the people against change from the customs and traditions of Judaism to faith of Christianity. Today the Gentile Church is no different. Many resent God's making a new covenant with Israel. We seem to forget that God is Sovereign.

We are now living in the Age of Grace, and unless we are obedient to the Lord Jesus Christ, we will be lost. The Jew also is presently living in the Age of Grace, and the same conditions apply to both Jew and Gentile during this age.

After the rapture of the Church, and during this week of tribulation (the last seven years of this age), God will deal particularly with Israel in the manner described by Paul and many other prophets.

In the Scripture above from Isaiah 66:7-10, the prophet is speaking of an end to the sins of Israel in Jerusalem, in a day when "those that are left" are few. This indicates that many of the Israelites will not be in Jerusalem due to the "time of Jacob's trouble" and the tribulation period during this last seven years of prophetic fulfillment. Of those that are left, he says, "This nation will be born in a day." Isaiah prophesied this by inspiration of the Holy Spirit; we can accept it as Truth. This prophecy has reference to the sins of Israel and God's new covenant with them. They (all of Israel that are left) will be saved from these sins when the Messiah returns to convert the nation in a day.

In the prophecy that we read from the thirty-sixth chapter of Ezekiel, we find that Ezekiel the prophet is speaking to the children of Israel. He is speaking concerning their restoration to God's favor and in the land. For many years some New Testament Christians have mistakenly been taught that the Old Testament is not profitable for instruction in righteousness and for giving to us the knowledge of God's will. However, the Bible is one book, and its teachings have to be harmonized. God's plan for His people, the Jews, and the world was not thwarted when Jesus came and brought the good news of the Gospel.

Both the Old Testament and the New Testament teach of God's dealings with Israel and with the Gentile nations. We need to study this more thoroughly. When Paul said, "All scripture is given by inspiration of God," he was speaking of the Old Testament as well as the New. In fact, Paul was at that point writing some of the New Testament. If we are aware of what God has said concerning the Jew in the Old Testament, and we harmonize that with what He says in the New Testament, then we can know that He is going to do some great and marvelous things in the near future.

Scripture teaches that He is going to make an end of sin concerning Israel and Jerusalem. This has never before been done. Those who accept Christ as their Savior in this age, both Jew and Gentile, will be forgiven of their sins. However, Israel alone has never been the object of an exclusive cleansing from sin. This will be accomplished at the second advent, with the coming of Christ to earth. The Scriptures say, "They shall see Him whom they have pierced."

In Scripture God said, "I will put my Spirit upon them [the nation of Israel]." God says the Spirit of repentance will be poured out upon Israel. Those who try to turn the

Scriptures into figurative puzzles and "spiritualize away" its literal meaning are making a great mistake. God says exactly what He means in simple truth so that the youngest and most inexperienced of His children can understand His direction.

God says to Israel, "There will be a fountain time." He says to Israel, "I will sprinkle clean water upon you." Many denominations of churches today use that as a "proof text" for baptism by sprinkling. However, God was not speaking to the *Church* in the Age of Grace; He was not speaking about the act of Christian immersion. He was speaking about a saving act that He would make specifically appropriate for the Jewish nation when *they* are restored in Palestine, at the end of the Age.

The purpose of the new covenant with Israel is to make reconciliation—atonement for their iniquity. For the Age of the Gentile, this was done on the cross for Israel and all other nations. You will recall, however, that Israel, as a nation rejected Jesus. Although a few Jews believed in Jesus and followed Him, the Jewish nation, as a people rejected Him and crucified Him.

When the disciples went out to preach, they were commanded to preach first to the Jew and then to the Gentile. They did this for a period of years, and finally, being convinced that the Jews would not accept the lordship of Christ, Paul said, "Lo, we turn to the Gentiles." From that time until now the preaching of the Gospel has been given primarily to the Gentile nations. The Jews will never be totally reconciled to God until Jesus appears to them as the One they have pierced, the Messiah they have rejected, when He comes to the earth the second time.

Daniel reminds us that the fourth purpose of this period (the last seven years of the age) is, "To bring in everlasting righteousness." At the time this takes place the Jews remaining after the Tribulation will be few in number. They will be a remnant, however, that will never again turn against God.

Everlasting righteousness will be their portion. This concerns only Israel.

Many Scriptures teach this, one example of which is Isaiah, chapter 9, verses 6 and 7:

> For unto us a child is born, unto us a son is given: and the government shall be upon his shoulder: and his name shall be called Wonderful, Counsellor, The mighty God, the everlasting Father, The Prince of Peace.
>
> Of the increase of his government and peace there shall be no end, upon the throne of David, and upon his kingdom, to order it, and to establish it with judgment and with justice from henceforth even for ever. The zeal of the Lord of hosts will perform this.

The first part of that prophecy has come true—a child was born and a son was given. However, the rest of that prophecy has not yet been fulfilled. It will be fulfilled when the prophecies of Daniel, chapter 2, verses 44 and 45, come true:

> And in the days of these kings shall the God of heaven set up a kingdom, which shall never be destroyed: and the kingdom shall not be left to other people, but it shall break in pieces and consume all these kingdoms, and it shall stand for ever.
>
> Forasmuch as thou sawest that the stone was cut out of the mountain without hands, and that it brake in pieces the iron, the brass, the clay, the silver, and the gold; the great God hath made known to the king what shall come to pass hereafter; and the dream is certain, and the interpretation thereof sure.

This Scripture speaks of the kingdom that Christ will usher in. Many contend that Christ ushered in this kingdom when the Church was born on Pentecost. However, the Bible says, "Flesh and blood cannot inherit the kingdom of God," and the men who were present and took part in and were saved in that great day were all mortal men. The kingdom that Jesus will usher in is a kingdom that will break in pieces all the nations of the world. The Church has been in existence for two thousand years, and it is a long way from fulfilling that prophecy.

The Church is not the kingdom that the Jews were expecting to be set up with the coming of the Messiah. The Church did not become that kingdom when Jesus sent the Holy Spirit to us on the day of Pentecost. The Bible tells us that after His resurrection Jesus spent forty days with His disciples teaching them about the kingdom of God. Just before He ascended into heaven, His disciples gathered around and said, "Lord, will thou at this time restore the kingdom?" Jesus said, "It is not for you to know the times or the seasons that God will do this." No one can predict when God will restore the kingdom. It is in His power alone.

The disciples were still expecting a visible kingdom with Jesus as the king. Jesus Himself prophesied that He would not eat or drink with these people again or see them again until He came to be with them in the future kingdom. He is not visibly present in the spiritual aspect of the kingdom, which we know as the Church. Therefore we may conclude that the Church is not that to which He had reference.

Everlasting righteousness will begin when the Lord comes at the end of this period of time (the last seven years of the age), with ten thousand of His saints. Enoch prophesied this three thousand years before the first advent of Jesus. If the Lord is going to come *with* ten thousand of His saints to bring in everlasting righteousness and the golden age upon the earth, and to rule as King of kings and Lord of lords, He has to come *for* them—in the Rapture event—before He can come *with* them.

The fifth event to occur when this time comes to pass (the last seven years of the age) is the sealing up of the prophecy. The literal rendering of "the seal of the prophets" is that there will be no more need for prophets to come to the nation of Israel. Prophecy then will be done. There will then be no more need for men to teach one another, because the word of the Lord will go forth from Jerusalem and the law of the Lord from Mount Zion. This will be done by the Lord. The righteousness of the Messiah will reign, and the Bible says, "For all shall know the Lord from the least to the greatest of them."

In Isaiah 11:9, the prophet has this to say:

> They shall not hurt nor destroy in all my holy mountain: for the earth shall be full of the knowledge of the Lord, as the waters cover the sea.

In the book of Jeremiah, chapter 31, verses 31 through 40, we read these words:

> Behold the days come, saith the Lord, that I will make a new covenant with the house of Israel, and with the house of Judah:
>
> Not according to the covenant that I made with their fathers in the day that I took them by the hand to bring them out of the land of Egypt; which my covenant they brake, although I was an husband unto them, saith the Lord:
>
> But this shall be the covenant that I will make with the house of Israel; after those days, saith the Lord, I will put my law in their inward parts, and write it in their hearts; and will be their God, and they shall be my people.
>
> And they shall teach no more every man his neighbour, and every man his brother, saying, Know the Lord: for they all shall know me, from the least of them unto the greatest of them, saith the Lord: for I will forgive their iniquity, and I will remember their sin no more.
>
> Thus saith the Lord, which giveth the sun for a light by day, and the ordinances of the moon and of the stars for a light by night, which divideth the sea when the waves thereof roar; the Lord of Hosts is his name:
>
> If those ordinances depart from before me, saith the Lord, then the seed of Israel also shall cease from being a nation before me for ever.
>
> Thus saith the Lord; If heaven above can be measured, and the foundations of the earth searched out beneath, I will also cast off all the seed of Israel for all that they have done, saith the Lord.

> Behold, the days come, saith the Lord, that the city shall be built to the Lord from the tower of Hananeel unto the gate of the corner.
>
> And the measuring line shall yet go forth over against it upon the hill Gareb, and shall compass about to Goath.
>
> And the whole valley of the dead bodies, and of the ashes, and all the fields unto the brook of Kidron, unto the corner of the horse gate toward the east, shall be holy unto the Lord; it shall not be plucked up, nor thrown down any more for ever.

Again in the book of Isaiah, chapter 66, verses 7 through 10, the prophet says this:

> Before she travailed, she brought forth; before her pain came, she was delivered of a man child.
>
> Who hath heard such a thing? who hath seen such things? Shall the earth be made to bring forth in one day? or shall a nation be born at once? for as soon as Zion travailed, she brought forth children.
>
> Shall I bring to the birth, and not cause to bring forth? saith the Lord: shall I cause to bring forth, and shut the womb? saith thy God.
>
> Rejoice ye with Jerusalem, and be glad with her, all ye that love her: rejoice for joy with her, all ye that mourn for her.

The last three verses above speak of the rebirth of the nation of Israel. It will come to pass much like a woman in childbirth travails before she brings forth her child.

These Scriptures say that God will make a new covenant with the house of Israel. Many people have misinterpreted this promise. They believe God is speaking of making a covenant with the Gentiles by the preaching of the Gospel. We must remember, however, that God deals with three different groups of people—the Gentiles, the Church, and the nation of Israel. This covenant, spoken of by the prophets, is with the nation of Israel. We must not attempt to change the meaning of the Scripture to suit our own purposes.

This new covenant with the house of Israel will last forever. It will not be according to the covenant made with Abraham or Moses or any of the early patriarchs. It will be a *new* covenant for the house of Israel. God is dealing with the time when Israel is once more a nation united and in possession of the promised land, and all prophecy of the new covenant hinges on this event.

All prophecies of the end of time rest upon the fact that Israel must be in possession of Jerusalem. Today Israel is in possession of the Holy City, and they will never willingly release it. The land has been forced from them, and they from the land, but they have never, nor will they ever, *willingly* relinquish possession.

Before the end of that seven-year period of tribulation, they will lose it for a while, but God has promised that eventually and eternally the land will be theirs.

One more event will take place during these seven years of tribulation—"To anoint the Most Holy." This refers to the cleansing of the temple that will be rebuilt in Jerusalem. Prior to this the temple will have been defiled with the "abomination of desolation," which will make necessary this cleansing. The meaning of the abomination of desolation is when, in the midst of the last seven years of the age (halfway through the last seven years), the antichrist will turn against the Jews, reneging on any promises to them or covenants he might have made with them. He will go into the temple and set himself up as God. We read of this in II Thessalonians 2:3-4:

> Let no man deceive you by any means: for that day shall not come, except there come a falling away first, and that man of sin be revealed, the son of perdition:
> Who opposeth and exalteth himself above all that is called God, or that is worshipped; so that he as God sitteth in the temple of God, shewing himself that he is God.

The antichrist is that man of iniquity—the man of sin. This prophecy will be accomplished in the middle of the week of years (three and a half literal years) before the end of the age.

There will be a time to cleanse the temple before the end of the age. This will be necessary due to the desecration brought upon it by the antichrist's proclaiming himself to be God.

Let us review the things we have studied thus far. The seventy weeks (weeks of years) of Daniel's prophecy began with the command to restore and rebuild the temple, when the children of Israel were in captivity under the Persian kings, Cyrus and Darius. Forty-nine years passed from the going forth of the decree to rebuild the temple until it was actually completed.

The crucifixion of the Messiah brought to an end the second period of fulfillment, which consisted of 434 years. Up to this point 483 literal years (six weeks of years), or all but one week of years (seven literal years), of Daniel's prophecy have been fulfilled. The Church Age in which we are now living is that period that Luke records Simeon speaking of. It precedes the last seven years of the age. In Acts, chapter 15, verses 13 through 17, we find James speaking these words:

> And after they had held their peace, James answered, saying, Men and brethren, hearken unto me:
> Simeon hath declared how God at the first did visit the Gentiles, to take out of them a people for his name.
> And to this agree the words of the prophets; as it is written,
> After this I will return, and will build again the tabernacle of David, which is fallen down; and I will build again the ruins thereof, and I will set it up:
> That the residue of men might seek after the Lord, and all the Gentiles, upon whom my name is called, saith the Lord, who doeth all these things.

Studying the background of this Scripture, Paul and Barnabas have followed Peter in his argument for Christian liberty, recounting how God is blessing the Gentiles without their having to keep the Jewish Law (the laws of Moses). Paul and Barnabas have confirmed the Word of God among the Gentiles, and

James argues that the prophets agree on the salvation of the Gentiles without keeping the Law.

The Jerusalem council was in session because Peter had gone unto the Gentiles for the conversion of Cornelius, and he had eaten with them. It is forbidden for a Jew to sit down at a Gentile's table, so Peter came under criticism by his fellow followers of Christ. At this time Jesus had already given the command to go into all the world and preach the gospel, baptizing those who believed. However, the early Church was very bigoted. It would not allow a Gentile to be part of the Church for several years. These early prejudices are much like those we see in many of our churches today.

Peter rehearsed the conversion of Cornelius. The tenth chapter of Matthew records the vision God sent to Peter, and at the same time he sent a vision to Cornelius. These visions from God brought the two men, Jew and Gentile, together. As Peter preached the gospel to the Gentiles, the Holy Spirit fell upon them, and Peter said, "Who can forbid water that these should be baptized who have received the Holy Spirit as well as we." The door of the Church was open to the Gentiles on that day. Jesus had fulfilled His prophecy concerning Peter, "Upon this rock I will build my Church."

In the Scripture above, James is saying that Peter has revealed to him that God sent him to the Gentiles to call out of them a people for His name. This was the beginning of the "Church Age." The people that are being called out of the Gentile nations today are members of the Church whom we call Christians. This "calling out" of a people for God is the reason we are to go into all the world and preach the Gospel. "He that believeth and is baptized shall be saved. He that believeth not shall be condemned."

God is at this time, through the preaching of the Gospel, taking out of the Gentile nations a people for His name, while He tarries in grace and mercy. We wear His name. This is the purpose of evangelism. He said, "After this [after this taking out of the nations a people for His name] I will return. I will build again the tabernacle of David. I will set it up that the rest of the Gentiles might seek after me."

In Scripture we studied earlier is the prophecy, "*All* shall know me from the least of them to the greatest of them." Everyone shall know God because the word of the Lord and the law of the Lord will go forth from Jerusalem and from Mount Zion itself. The teaching of the Word at that time will no longer be hindered by the lawlessness and rebellion of man against God or by man's inadequacies.

We have covered briefly the 70 weeks of the prophecy of Daniel and studied how it relates only to the nation of Israel. We see that 483 years of these prophecies have already been fulfilled. They were fulfilled at the crucifixion of Jesus, when the Messiah was cut off in death, as the Scripture teaches.

The last seven years of the prophecy of Daniel are awaiting the gleanings from the Gentile nations of the world by the preaching of the Gospel. As the Church goes forth and preaches and witnesses in the name of Jesus, it takes out of the nations a people for His name, and thus fulfills that prophecy of the Old Testament.

II

The Rapture of the Church

The event which today we call "the Rapture of the Church" was known in early New Testament times, during the first four centuries, as "Chilaism." This was the prominent doctrine of the Church concerning the second coming of Jesus, until the formation of the state church in the empire of Rome. Irenius, one of the early church fathers, then declared the doctrine of Chilaism to be erroneous, a misinterpretation of Scripture. From that time the Church fathers began to mysticize the literal Scripture teachings that pertained to the second coming of the Lord and the Rapture of the Church.

The "Rapture" of which we speak simply means the catching up, or the snatching away of all true believers in Christ (both the dead and the living) to meet the Lord in the air. This event is reserved for the Church only.

In I Thessalonians, Paul writes concerning one of the problems about which the Thessalonian Christians had questioned him. They were concerned about the deaths of some of the early Church brethren before Jesus returned. He writes to correct the impression that their loved ones were lost forever. In I Thessalonians 4:13-18 we read what Paul has to say:

> But I would not have you to be ignorant, brethren, concerning them which are asleep, that ye sorrow not, even as others which have no hope.
>
> For if we believe that Jesus died and rose again, even so them also which sleep in Jesus will God bring with him.
>
> For this we say unto you by the word of the Lord, that we which remain unto the coming of the Lord shall not precede them which are asleep.

For the Lord himself shall descend from heaven with a shout, with the voice of the archangel, and with the trump of God: and the dead in Christ shall rise first:

Then we which are alive and remain shall be caught up together with them in the clouds, to meet the Lord in the air: and so shall we ever be with the Lord.

Wherefore comfort one another with these words.

This Scripture is read more often at funerals than at any other time. Due to the sadness of such an event, its true meaning is clouded, and the listener is unaware of what Paul is saying to us.

If we determine who is speaking and to whom he is speaking, for what purpose he is speaking, and to whom it applies, then we must say that Paul is speaking to the Christians. He is speaking concerning the coming of the Lord from heaven, for saints, dead and living, in order that they may be joined together with Him forever in the air. This was written to bring comfort to the sorrowing Thessalonians who believed that their dead saints, who had passed on before this, were gone forever.

In the fifteenth chapter of I Corinthians, which we commonly call the resurrection chapter, the apostle Paul speaks of the resurrections in the twenty-third verse. He says, "But every man in his own order;" the word for order used here is *tagma*. It is the Greek word that is designated as a military order meaning rank by rank, in an orderly fashion.

Every man in his own order, Christ the first fruits, afterwards they that are Christ's at his coming. Then, after this, cometh the end when He shall have delivered up the kingdom to God, even the Father, when He shall have put down all rule, all authority and power, for He must reign till He hath put all enemies under His feet.

The twentieth chapter of Revelation indicates that Christ's reign is on the earth for a thousand years. In verses 51 through 58 in I Corinthians 15, Paul writes the following to the Church:

Behold, I shew you a mystery; We shall not all sleep, but we shall all be changed,

In a moment, in the twinkling of an eye, at the last trump: for the trumpet shall sound, and the dead shall be raised incorruptible, and we shall be changed.

For this corruptible must put on incorruption, and this mortal must put on immortality.

So when this corruptible shall have put on incorruption, and this mortal shall have put on immortality, then shall be brought to pass the saying that is written, Death is swallowed up in victory.

O death, where is thy sting? O grave, where is thy victory?

The sting of death is sin; and the strength of sin is the law.

But thanks be to God, which giveth us the victory through our Lord Jesus Christ.

Therefore, my beloved brethren, be ye stedfast, unmoveable, always abounding in the work of the Lord, forasmuch as ye know that your labour is not in vain in the Lord.

In Philippians, chapter 3 and in verses 20 and 21, Paul says again to the Christians:

For our conversation [citizenship] is in heaven from whence also we look for our Savior, the Lord Jesus Christ,

Who shall change our vile body that it may be fashioned like unto His glorious body, according to the working whereby He is able even to subdue all things unto himself.

In all of the above Scripture, please note that the resurrection of the wicked dead has not been mentioned. Nor has mention been made of the living wicked. The wicked of the earth have no part in the Rapture of the Church.

There is another portion of Scripture that is familiar to us, also used more often in funerals, and we tend to overlook what Jesus is saying to His disciples. This is John 14:2-3:

In my father's house are many mansions [or dwelling places]: if it were not so, I would have told you. I go to prepare a place for you;

And if I go to prepare a place for you, I will come again to receive you unto myself; that where I am, there you may be also.

In the twenty-first chapter of the Gospel of Luke, in verses 34 through 36, Jesus said this, concerning the end-time events that will come upon the believer in the world:

Take heed to yourselves, lest at any time your hearts be overcharged with surfeiting, and drunkenness, and cares of this life, and so that day come upon you unawares.
For as a snare shall it come on all them that dwell on the face of the whole earth.
Watch ye therefore, and pray always, that ye may be accounted worthy to escape all these things that shall come to pass, and to stand before the Son of man.

The things that Jesus speaks of as coming to pass are all these events that are listed as "end-time signs." He promises that the faithful, if they watch and pray, will be accounted worthy to escape all these things.

In Colossians, chapter 3, and in verse 4, we find these words:

When Christ, who is our life, shall appear, then shall ye also appear with Him in Glory.

This means that Christians are going to appear with Jesus before the throne of God in Glory. He is speaking not only to the Colossian Christians, but to the Christians of today, and all the Christians of all the centuries that separate us from the time of Christ.

Our study of these passages will prove that there is actually to be an event, such as the Lord descending from Heaven, and taking out of the graves all of the righteous dead, and catching away (the Greek word is *harpazo*, which means snatching up suddenly) all of the living saints to be with Him. The

Scriptures tell us that He will accomplish this in a moment, in the twinkling of an eye, and we shall appear with Him before God in glory.

It may be difficult for some to understand how this will be accomplished. However, the Bible is clear when it says, "Then we which are alive and remain shall be caught up together with them [with the resurrected dead saints] in the clouds."

In the Scriptures the Rapture is called "the coming of the Lord." It is never referred to as the second *visible* coming of Jesus to the earth. He is coming for His own people. At the Rapture of the Church, Jesus does not appear visibly to the people on the earth, but He will call Christians up, with the sound of a trumpet. This is not the last trumpet, or the seventh trumpet of Revelation. This trumpet call in the Rapture is the marching order, or the assembly call of the trumpet of God, for the sons of God on earth.

Many Scriptures have been misapplied to one or the other comings of Jesus to the world. Examining some of these, we shall try to understand why there seems to be such difficulty of interpretation in this matter.

The Rapture of the Church is a New Testament doctrine only. It was not taught in the Old Testament due to the fact that the Church was not revealed at the time of its writing. Paul first introduced the doctrine of the Rapture in the fifteenth chapter of the first Corinthian letter, which is believed by many teachers to be the first book written concerning the New Testament dispensation.

The second coming of Christ, however, is not limited to a New Testament doctrine. Much of the Old Testament is concerned with His visible appearance to the earth the second time to take over the reins of government in Israel on the earth. The Old Testament prophets never saw the New Testament Church in prophecy, and yet Jesus spoke of its coming in the future in Matthew 16:18, when He says to Peter, "Upon this rock I will build my church." The Church of which He spoke was revealed on Pentecost. Paul spoke of it in his inspired writings, and it is still in existence today.

The Rapture should never be called the second coming of Christ. This is His secret coming for the Church. He will not then be visible to wicked men on earth. He will not even be visible from the earth to the saints. In a moment those who are ready, waiting and watching will be caught up with the trumpet sound, all to be forever with the Lord in the air.

As we have noted in other passages, when Paul says, "We shall be changed in a moment, in the twinkling of an eye," it will be very sudden and quick. This is why we are told in I John 2:3 to purify ourselves even as He is pure, and be constantly ready for the Lord's return for us. There is nothing to prevent the Lord's coming for His Church at any time. From the time He left the earth, until now, He could have come back at any moment.

There are no "signs" that must precede the coming of the Lord for the Church. There are signs, however, that must precede His coming back to the earth *with* the Church. We shall study about these signs in a later chapter. The only indication we are given of the situation in which men of the earth will be found just prior to the Rapture is given in II Timothy 3:1-5:

> This know also, that in the last days perilous times shall come.
> For men shall be lovers of their own selves, covetous, boasters, proud, blasphemers, disobedient to parents, unthankful, unholy,
> Without natural affection, trucebreakers, false accusers, incontinent, fierce, despisers of those that are good,
> Traitors, heady, highminded, lovers of pleasures more than lovers of God;
> Having a form of godliness, but denying the power thereof; from such turn away.

This sounds very similar to a description of the condition of our world today.

There is a period of seven years between the coming of

Christ for the Church (the Rapture), and His coming in great power and judgment, to begin His judgment of the living nations described in the twenty-fifth chapter of Matthew, and His rule and reign upon the earth predicted so long ago by Isaiah and the other prophets.

There is not found one passage of Scripture referring to both of these events, His secret coming for the Church and His visible appearing to rule, as being one single event. They are separate. The first is secret and for those who are waiting and have been saved, and who are faithful and steadfast. It is a secret coming. The other appearance is visible, and every eye shall see and behold Him, and everyone on the earth will know that He is indeed Lord of lords and King of kings.

The world will scarcely be aware in many localities that the Rapture of the Church has taken place and that the Christians of the earth have been taken to be with Christ. The Scriptures teach us that when Christ comes back to the earth the second time, He comes with all His saints. If He is to come *with* all of His saints in the second visible advent, then He must come *for* them at some time preceding this visible appearance to the earth.

The Scriptures teach that the saints are in heaven before God from the time of the Rapture until the time of their coming again to reign as kings and priests with Jesus. In the book of Jude, verses 14 and 15 we read:

> And Enoch also, the seventh from Adam, prophesied of these, saying, Behold, the Lord cometh with ten thousands of his saints,
> To execute judgment upon all, and to convince all that are ungodly among them of all their ungodly deeds which they have ungodly committed, and of all their hard speeches which ungodly sinners have spoken against him.

Also, in the book of Revelation, chapter 19, verse 14 we read:

And the armies which were in heaven followed him upon white horses, clothed in fine linen, white and clean.

These passages of Scripture above refer to the *visible* second advent of the Lord with the armies of heaven and with ten thousands of His saints. The Scriptures teach that the saints are judged and given their rewards, after the Rapture, preceding the second visible coming of Jesus to the earth, when they shall return with Him.

From the beginning of the fourth chapter of the book of Revelation, up to verse 14 in chapter 19, the Church is absent from the earth. The Church is not mentioned as being on earth at all in the events between chapter 4 and chapter 19. In Revelation 19:14 is the first mention of the Church since it disappeared from view in the latter part of the third chapter of Revelation. Here in Revelation 19:14 we find the Church as the armies of God, already in heaven. The coming of Jesus with the armies of heaven will include His angels and all the redeemed of all the ages.

In II Corinthians, chapter 5:9 and 10, we read, "Wherefore we labor that whether present [living] or absent [dead] we may be accepted of Him." Speaking again of the Church he says, "For we must all appear before the judgment seat of Christ, that everyone [every member] may receive the things done in this body, according to that he has done whether it be good or bad."

The believer, having been saved and raptured, appears at the judgment seat of Christ where his works are judged. At that time he will receive his rewards according to his works. The judgment seat of Christ is not a general judgment of all people on the earth as is commonly believed. This is a judgment of Christians only. We may come to this conclusion because Paul is writing only to Christians. He is writing to those who are to be present with the Lord. They have been raptured from the earth, and those that are with the Lord must appear before the judgment seat of Christ.

The time a Christian spends before the judgment seat of Christ will be a time of terror for many. The apostle said, "Knowing therefore the terror of the Lord, we persuade men." It will be a time when every idle word, every thought and deed and careless act that every Christian has ever committed will be brought out into the white hot light of the holiness and purity of God. Every Christian's reward will be determined by this judgment. It behooves us, therefore, to be clear in conscience and mind, and in our dealings with one another in Christ, that we not stand before Him at the judgment seat of Christ, in shame and terror.

At His second visible advent, Christ departs from heaven, and He comes to earth. He does not come from the air above the earth. The Bible says He departs from heaven. In the nineteenth chapter of Revelation, verses 11 through 21, Christ is departing from heaven to come down to earth. John says:

> And I saw heaven opened, and behold a white horse; and he that sat upon him was called Faithful and True, and in righteousness he doth judge and make war.
>
> His eyes were as a flame of fire, and on his head were many crowns; and he had a name written, that no man knew, but he himself.
>
> And he was clothed with a vesture dipped in blood: and his name is called the Word of God.
>
> And the armies which were in heaven followed him upon white horses, clothed in fine linen, white and clean.
>
> And out of his mouth goeth a sharp sword, that with it he should smite the nations: and he shall rule them with a rod of iron: and he treadeth the winepress of the fierceness and wrath of Almighty God.
>
> And he hath on his vesture and on his thigh a name written, KING OF KINGS, AND LORD OF LORDS.
>
> And I saw an angel standing in the sun; and he cried with a loud voice, saying to all the fowls that fly in the midst of heaven, Come and gather yourselves together unto the supper of the great God;
>
> That ye may eat the flesh of kings, and the flesh of captains, and the flesh of mighty men, and the flesh of horses, and of

them that sit on them, and the flesh of all men, both free and bond, both small and great.

And I saw the beast, and the kings of the earth, and their armies, gathered together to make war against him that sat on the horse, and against his army.

And the beast was taken, and with him the false prophet that wrought miracles before him, with which he deceived them that had received the mark of the beast, and them that worshipped his image. These both were cast alive into a lake of fire burning with brimstone.

And the remnant were slain with the sword of him that sat upon the horse, which sword proceeded out of his mouth: and all the fowls were filled with their flesh.

Another Scripture that is profitable to study in connection with this subject is the second letter Paul wrote to the Thessalonian Christians (II Thessalonians 1:7-10):

And to you who are troubled rest with us, when the Lord Jesus shall be revealed from heaven with his mighty angels,

In flaming fire taking vengeance on them that know not God, and that obey not the gospel of our Lord Jesus Christ:

Who shall be punished with everlasting destruction from the presence of the Lord, and from the glory of his power;

When he shall come to be glorified in his saints, and to be admired in all them that believe (because our testimony among you was believed) in that day.

Please keep in mind that Paul is referring to Christ's second visible advent, and not the Rapture of the Church. These Scriptures tell of the visible coming of Christ to all of the world, when He shall be revealed from heaven with His mighty angels, in flaming fire, taking vengeance on them that know not God and who obey not the gospel of our Lord Jesus Christ.

In II Thessalonians, chapter 2 and in verse 1 we have a different aspect. Here we have Him speaking of our appearance, following the Rapture of the Church. This speaks of our appearance *with* Him.

Now we beseech you, brethren, by the coming of our Lord Jesus Christ, and by our gathering together unto Him.

The Church is going to be gathered together unto the Lord. This is a promise for the Church only. The Rapture must take place and Christ must first come for the Church secretly, as a thief in the night, before He can come with them visibly as the armies of heaven, with all of the saints in judgment upon the earth.

At the Rapture of the Church, the Lord comes from heaven as far as the earthly atmosphere, and out of sight of the wicked world. He will catch the Church up to Him. In the second visible advent, He comes down to earth from heaven and destroys His adversaries in judgment and fire.

In the book of Luke, chapter 21, verses 34 through 36, we read these words:

And take heed to yourselves, lest at any time your hearts be overcharged with surfeiting, and drunkenness, and cares of this life, and so that day come upon you unawares.

For as a snare shall it come on all them that dwell on the face of the whole earth.

Watch ye therefore, and pray always, that ye may be accounted worthy to escape all these things that shall come to pass, and to stand before the Son of man.

In John 14:3 Jesus says:

And if I go to prepare a place for you, I will come again, and receive you unto myself; that where I am, there ye may be also.

In I Corinthians 15:13 the Bible tells us:

But if there be no resurrection of the dead, then is Christ not risen.

In Ephesians 5:27 the Apostle Paul says:

That he might present it to himself a glorious church, not having spot, or wrinkle, or any such thing; but that it should be holy and without blemish.

In Philippians 3:20 he says:

For our conversation [citizenship] is in heaven; from whence also we look for the Saviour, the Lord Jesus Christ.

In I Thessalonians 4:16 we read:

For the Lord himself shall descend from heaven with a shout, with the voice of the archangel, and with the trump of God: and the dead in Christ shall rise first.

In II Thessalonians 2:1 and 7 and 8 we read these words:

Now we beseech you, brethren, by the coming of our Lord Jesus Christ, and by our gathering together unto him,

*   *   *

For the mystery of iniquity doth already work: only he who now letteth will let, until he be taken out of the way.
And then shall that wicked be revealed, whom the Lord shall consume with the spirit of his mouth, and shall destroy with the brightness of his coming.

In these Scriptures Paul speaks of the mystery of iniquity already at work in the world, that will extend throughout the Church Age. There will be a rapid increase in the times of the end. That rapid increase of lawlessness is synonymous with the great apostasy and the lukewarmness and the complacency of the Church. When the Scriptures say, "Until *he* be taken out of the way," reference is not made to the Lord Jesus Christ; neither is the Scripture referring to the Holy Spirit. The Holy Spirit will be present during the tribulation period in the same manner that He was present in the Old Testament. Paul is speaking of the Body of Christ, which is the only real hinderer of lawlessness in the world today. The Body of Christ in the world today is the Church.

Governments do not hinder lawlessness or iniquity; the devil does not hinder lawlessness or iniquity. The Holy Spirit hinders lawlessness through the Church, which is the body of Christ. When the body of Christ, the *true* Church, is gone from the earth, there will be a tremendous increase in iniquity, due to the lack of religious or spiritual influence on the earth. The "World Church," which will come on the scene during the last seven years of the age, will not be of such a nature as to hinder iniquity and lawlessness. This "World Church" will no doubt be made up of many people who have their names on church rolls, but who are not true, born-again Christians.

The reason we have referred to the body of Christ as "he" when we speak of the taking of the Church out of the world is simply this: Christ was a man. Therefore, we can refer to the Church, which is His body, in the masculine gender. I believe that this is the "he" referred to by the Apostle.

It is to the shame of the Church today that there are many people who wear the ministerial cloth that no longer believe in the truth of the Bible or adhere to its teachings. Many of these people are heads of great church organizations. It is because many no longer believe in the authority of God, authority in the home, and the authority of Governments, that wickedness already prevails and abounds in the world. This is a condition that comes always upon men when there is a great falling away from the faith and disobedience to God's word.

What is the purpose of the Rapture? The purpose of the Rapture of the Church is to take the living righteous and the righteous dead from the earth together; to take all the saints out of the world *before* the tribulation (called in Scripture "the time of Jacob's trouble") comes upon the world. We shall study about this subject further in the next chapter.

Students of the book of Revelation will recognize that there are such plagues as war, famine and disturbances of nature mentioned in Scripture contained therein. Each time a plague is visited upon the earth the result will be death to a great number of people in the world. During this period of time (the last seven years of this age), the nation of Israel will undergo tribulation that is of such terrible nature that Scripture says that except those days be shortened, even the very elect would not be saved. The "elect" referred to here are those men and women who are still living in the nation of Israel. The Rapture will take the righteous in Christ away from the earth before the time of Jacob's trouble comes upon the world, so that the Church will not suffer such tribulation. Jesus says, "Pray that ye may be accounted worthy to escape all these things that shall come to pass on the earth, and to stand before the Son of Man."

The Rapture of the Church before the beginning of the last week of the prophecy of Daniel, which is the last seven years of the present age on this earth, is the first of a series of Raptures that will take place before Jesus comes visibly to the earth the second time. After the Church disappears from the earth (Revelation 3), in the resurrection order of Christ, as part of the first fruits of the resurrection, in the middle of the week (three and a half years), 144,000 Jews are marked from the twelve tribes of Israel. They are sealed in order that they may escape death from all the plagues of the tribulation to come. In the seventh chapter of Revelation, we see this 144,000 on the earth. Then, in Revelation, chapter 14, we see them in heaven. They've been Raptured during the tribulation period.

John then looks around the throne of God and sees a great multitude of martyred saints, and he says, "Who are they?" The angel who is with John replies, "They are those who have come out of the great tribulation and have had their robes washed white in the blood of the lamb." This teaches that there is also a great group of tribulation saints to be Raptured. These are people who will believe in and accept Jesus Christ between the time of the disappearance of the Church from the earth and the second coming of Jesus visibly to the earth, although it means that when they accept Him, or refuse to renounce Him, they will probably be killed.

These people cannot be thought to have been given a "second chance." If to bow the knee to Christ and to confess Him with the mouth before men, or to refuse to accept the authority of the antichrist in obedience to Jesus, means they will be slain, that is not the kind of "second chance" many would welcome.

The purpose of the Rapture of the Church is to take the saints who are ready and waiting out of the earth to miss the terrible conditions of the tribulation period. However, there are millions of people who do not study the Bible and do not know how they might escape the tribulation period. This is the purpose for God's allowing the Church to remain on the earth as long as He has—to witness to the earth and gather as many as will unto the fold of the Church.

Unfortunately, there are those who will not accept Christ unless some great tragedy comes into their lives that affects the entire family and draws them near the fact that there is an end to life, and that it could come very suddenly.

People who are saved during the tribulation period do not have a second chance. It means that they have put off accepting the salvation that Christ offers until, when they do accept it, they have already missed the joy of the first Rapture, and they will be put to death for their witness for Jesus. These are the tribulation saints that come out of great tribulation, who give their lives for their witness and the testimony of Jesus. John says they are a great multitude that no man can number.

If people will not be saved now with all the Gospel that is being preached, it's not likely that they will be saved as long as conditions continue as they are. Once men realize that God means what He says, because the Church is gone in Rapture from the earth, many will turn to Jesus Christ. The actual out-resurrection from the dead is not just of the dead at the Rapture of the Church, but it will also mean the catching up of the 144,000 Jews who are saved for special service to Christ, as well as a great multitude of tribulation saints who are martyred because of the wickedness of the antichrist, in that seven-year tribulation period at the end of this age.

Scripture says they will be resurrected in their own order, each at their own appointed time. These are the different ranks and companies: first the Church, then the 144,000, then the tribulation saints.

Jesus is coming to take the Church unto Himself, to judge the Church, and then present the Church to the Father. In order to be presented to God in glory, the bodies of all of the saints must be changed. From mortality we must be made to be immortal, so that we will have the same type of spiritual body that Christ has. The saints will be presented whole in body, soul and spirit before God. Man is a three-part entity—body, soul, and spirit. When Jesus comes and we are immediately translated and changed in a moment, in the twinkling of an eye, we will be made whole in body, soul, and spirit—a perfect spiritual man, even as Jesus is.

Many contend today that they do not understand the book of Revelation. However, it may not be altogether necessary for one to understand it. If you are already in Christ, and His word abides in you, you are going to miss all the events that come to pass on earth which are spoken of between chapters 6 and 19 of the book of Revelation. Jesus is going to come for us in the Rapture. This thought, though, should not make us complacent. We should be concerned about those who are going to miss the Rapture of the Church and who will have to stand in the tribulation period. It is because of this that we should strive to study and witness to those about us so that they, too, will be taken out of the terrible time that is to come very soon.

The wickedness and lawlessness of our world today goes

hand-in-hand with the figurative casting of the Word of God into the burial pit. For many people on this earth, God is already dead. Many people who claim to be God's children behave as though He is dead. They do not acknowledge that He is going to do any of these things. They are ignorant of His word.

Following the removal of the Church from the earth, the antichrist will be revealed. The Bible speaks of this man as coming from the nation of Syria (Old Testament Syria). In the book of Daniel, the prophet says that the antichrist will come from a nation that is not a very great nation in the eyes of the world, and this will take the nations by surprise.

Already in our economic system, and in the alignment of the different states of Europe, and in the oil problems that come to us from the nations of Asia, the process is working. In the first chapter of this study we quoted Daniel as saying that all of the problems that come during these 490 years of prophecy dealing with the Israelites have only been applicable to them when they have been gathered together in the land. From the time of the destruction of Jerusalem in A.D. 70 until 1948, they were dispersed into all the world. Since 1948 over three million of them have assembled in the land, and Israel has once more assumed her place in the family of nations, in accordance with the divine will of God, and in fulfillment of prophecy.

Even though the seventieth week of years has not yet begun, the nation of Israel is present in the family of nations. God is not a man, that He should lie. He keeps His word, and by this we may know that the last week of years—the last seven years of time—will soon come to pass. The most impressive thought in this connection is that there is nothing to prevent the Rapture of the Church from taking place now, or at any time. The Church could have been Raptured immediately following the preaching of Peter to Cornelius when the Gospel was first taken to the Gentiles. There are no unfulfilled prophecies to be accomplished before this event takes place.

Only the long suffering of God has prevented the Rapture

thus far. God will not allow Jesus to come and take the Church home prematurely because, Scripture says that He is not willing that any should perish, but that all might come to repentance. God desires that men might know the joys of being caught up in the air and escaping the tribulations that will come upon the world and bring an end to this age of the Church and the Gentile Age. When that happens, Jesus can usher in that rule of righteousness and universal peace that the prophets spoke of so long ago.

When Jesus' reign is established, "The nations shall not learn war any more. They shall beat their swords into plowshares, their spears into pruning hooks. A man shall sit under his own vine and fig tree." "He shall not build and another inherit. The life of a man will be as the life of a tree. A little child shall lead the wild beast of the forest. The lion and the lamb will lie down together."

All of these wonderful promises are for the golden age that will come upon the earth when Jesus is reigning, preceding the delivering of the kingdom up unto God, and the final destruction of that great prince of liars, Satan, himself. While we are waiting for these events, the Church could be Raptured any moment.

III

The Signs of the Times

There are foretold certain events that will concern the Jewish nation and those things that will come to pass upon the earth during the tribulation spoken of between the sixth and nineteenth chapters of the book of Revelation. If those fourteen chapters are read in connection with the twenty-fourth and twenty-fifth chapters of Matthew, we shall have to conclude that these signs are of Jewish origin; that Jesus is speaking to the disciples, answering their questions as they sought to know what would be the time of the end of the age, and of Jesus' return to the earth.

In the preceding chapter we studied the Rapture, or of the coming of the Lord for the Church secretly. In this chapter of the study, the signs of the second advent of Jesus, or His visible coming to earth will be presented.

Keep in mind that in the Rapture of the Church, He will not be appearing to people on the earth, but He will come in the air and catch away His Church secretly. Not until the end of the seven-year tribulation period will He come visibly with all the saints and the armies of heaven to the earth. Contained in the twenty-fourth and twenty-fifth chapters of the book of Matthew are prophecies of the things that happen between the Rapture of the Church and the visible return of Jesus to the earth.

At the beginning of Matthew 24 Jesus has just made this startling statement concerning the temple in Jerusalem:

> See ye not all these things? verily I say unto you, There shall not be left here one stone upon another, that shall not be thrown down.

47

This precipitated these questions from the disciples, which we find in Matthew 24:3:

> And as he sat upon the mount of Olives, the disciples came unto him privately, saying, Tell us, when shall these things be? and what shall be the sign of thy coming, and of the end of the world?

When the disciples looked out at that great and magnificent temple that had been built, they could hardly understand that it would be utterly and totally destroyed within forty years after Jesus spoke these words. The temple had nine gates overlaid with gold and silver. One gate was of solid Corinthian brass. There were towering porches, alternate blocks of red and white marble, vast clusters of golden grapes, each cluster being as large as a man, and each cluster hung over the golden doors.

The great stones in the temple were about fifty-two feet in length, and about sixteen feet in height and about twenty-five feet in breadth, and were laid one on top of the other in orderly fashion to form the great temple. Is it any wonder that the disciples found it rather difficult to believe that this magnificent structure would be utterly destroyed?

Concerning the second visible advent, Jesus said that the signs preceding it would begin with the destruction of the temple, which took place in A.D. 70. The signs of His second visible return to the earth began at that time, and in every generation since that time some of these signs have been present. There have always been wars and rumors of wars. Since that time the Jews have been severely persecuted, even in our own generation. There have been famines, and pestilences, and earthquakes in different places in the earth throughout the history of man.

In the last decade, pestilences have greatly increased. In the last two decades the "birth pangs" of Israel have increased a hundredfold. Earthquakes in the last ten years have increased two thousandfold over the previous listings recorded. There has been a marked increase of all of these signs in the last decade, but they are still not yet present in the intensity that Jesus said they would be just prior to His return to the earth.

False messiahs will appear before the end of the week. This leads us to believe that these signs are Jewish because the Gentiles have never looked for a Messiah. The Jews as a nation did not think that Jesus was the Messiah, so they are still looking for their "deliverer," thus opening the way to false messiahs and misled leaders.

In the middle of the week of years, the abomination of desolation, spoken of by Daniel the prophet, will take place in the temple. This will result in the literal taking over of the nation of Israel and all of the other nations already subdued by the antichrist. The antichrist will then set himself up as God in the temple, and he will cause men to worship his image and his idol, and bear the mark of his name and his number.

"There will be wars and rumors of wars." This condition has always been present in the world, but there will be a marked increase of these wars in this period of tribulation, after the Church is Raptured. Nation will rise against nation and there will be famines and pestilences and earthquakes. These events are foretold briefly in the twenty-fourth chapter of Matthew and in great detail in chapters six through nineteen of the book of Revelation.

Because these signs and that portion of the book of Revelation that we have just noted pertain to the Jewish people, all of the signs and symbols in that book are strictly Jewish. None of them apply to the Gentile Church, or to the Age of the Gentiles.

At this time the Jews will be severely persecuted by all the nations of the earth. The Bible teaches this. The Israeli presently have friends in several nations of the world, but in this week of years, after the Church is Raptured, they will have few friends. They will be persecuted by all nations because the nations will believe that it is because of the Jews that these problems they are experiencing have come. The Bible says that in that time many of the Jews will betray one another. As we look at the international situation today, we can see that many people would do away with the nation of Israel in order to bring peace to the Middle East, and in order to secure the great oil deposits and other mineral deposits that are in that area.

These things that are taking place today are only indications of the great and tremendous betrayals and offenses that they will work against one another not only in the nations of the world, but in the nation of Israel itself, in that week of years after the Church is Raptured from the earth.

During this time iniquity will abound upon the earth in a far greater sense than it does now. We are told that the love of many will wax cold. Many students of the Word relate this to the Church, and it can be applied to the Church today in a sense, because the love of many for Jesus is waxing cold. However, this statement is a prophetic prediction that applies to the Jewish nation. The love of many waxing cold is not necessarily the love of many for God, but the love of one Jew for another. This love will wax cold during the tribulation, and there will be great divisions and differences among the people in the nations.

The Bible says that the gospel of the kingdom will be preached to all the world as a witness to all nations. The "gospel of the kingdom" is not the gospel of grace. Jesus Christ has already come. He has already made a sacrifice for the redemption of sins of both Jew and Gentile. The gospel of the kingdom that will be preached during the seven years of tribulation before the second visible return to Jesus, will be the gospel of the kingdom that John the Baptist preached and that the disciples were commissioned to preach when they were sent out preaching unto Israel, "Repent, for the kingdom of heaven is at hand."

This gospel will again herald the coming of the Messiah. The gospel of the kingdom of heaven differs from the gospel of grace. The gospel of the kingdom will be preached in all of the world up to the middle of that seven years, as a witness unto all nations, and not necessarily to each person of all nations.

Following the preaching of the kingdom gospel, the abomination of desolation will be set up in the midst of the week of years. At this time many of the Jews will flee into the wilderness. In Matthew 24:16 we read, "Then let them which be in Judea flee into the mountains."

Isaiah, speaking of this time, says:

> Send ye the lamb to the ruler of the land from Sela to the wilderness, unto the mount of the daughter of Zion.
> For it shall be, that, as a wandering bird cast out of the nest, so the daughters of Moab shall be at the fords of Arnon.
> Take counsel, execute judgment; make thy shadow as the night in the midst of the noonday; hide the outcasts; bewray not him that wandereth.
> Let mine outcasts dwell with thee, Moab; be thou a covert to them from the face of the spoiler: for the extortioner is at an end, the spoiler ceaseth, the oppressors are consumed out of the land.
> And in mercy shall the throne be established: and he shall sit upon it in truth in the tabernacle of David, judging, and seeking judgment, and hasting righteousness. (Isaiah 16:1-5)

This prophecy simply states that Moab will give succor and shelter to the children of Israel when they flee from Jerusalem, when the antichrist sets himself up as God, in the throne room of the temple.

Isaiah continues in chapter 26, verses 20 and 21:

> Come, my people, enter thou into thy chambers, and shut thy doors about thee: hide thyself until the indignation be overpast.
> For, behold, the Lord cometh out of his place to punish the inhabitants of the earth for their iniquity: the earth also shall disclose her blood, and shall no more cover her slain.

Again in Isaiah, chapter 63, verses 1 through 5, the prophet says:

> Who is this that cometh from Edom, with dyed garments, from Bozrah? This that is glorious in his apparel, traveling in the greatness of his strength? I that speak in righteousness, mighty to save.
> Wherefore art thou red in thine apparel, and thy garments like him that treadeth in the winefat?
> I have trodden the winepress alone; and of the people there was none with me: for I will tread them in mine anger, and trample them in my fury; and their blood shall be sprinkled upon my garments, and I will stain all my raiment.
> For the day of vengeance is in mine heart, and the year of my redeemed is come.
> And I looked, and there was none to help; and I wondered that there was none to uphold: therefore mine own arm brought salvation unto me; and my fury, it upheld me.

The basic teaching of these Old Testament scriptures is this: the Jewish people who are still alive at this time will be sheltered, some of them perhaps, in the rock of Petra, there protected by some of the Arab nations, or the people of Moab and Bozrah. They will be hidden there, safe from the power of the antichrist when Jesus comes with all of His saints, to set up His rule on the earth. They will be able to see Him as He comes from the east and passes over them. We have every evidence in Scripture to prove that.

Now let us note what Ezekiel says in chapter 20, verses 33 and 34:

> As I live, saith the Lord God, surely with a mighty hand, and with a stretched out arm, and with fury poured out, will I rule over you:
> And I will bring you out from the people, and will gather you out of the countries wherein ye are scattered, with a mighty hand, and with a stretched out arm, and with fury poured out.

From this Scripture we learn that when the Lord comes, one of the first tasks that He will perform will be the gathering of the remnant of Israel—a remnant of the people that escaped from the antichrist, when he set up his power in Jerusalem in the middle of the seven years. These will have taken shelter in the rock city of Petra under the protectorship of Moab and Bozrah. Jesus will gather the people out into the wilderness from the nations and purge those that are the rebellious ones. Only those who recognize Him as the Son of God will enter into Jerusalem with Him.

Hosea speaks of this when he says,

> Therefore, behold, I will allure her, and bring her into the wilderness, and speak comfortably unto her.
> And I will give her her vineyards from thence, and the valley of Achor for a door of hope; and she shall sing there, as in the days of her youth, and as in the day when she came up out of the land of Egypt. (Hosea 2:14-15)

The Lord speaks of blessing them, and breaking the bow and the sword and the battle out of the earth, and making them lie down safely. "Betroth thee Israel unto me forever, betroth thee unto me in righteousness and in judgment and in loving-kindness." Here He is speaking of the sphere of eternal righteousness and lovingkindness that the Lord will give the Jewish people, when they come back from hiding from the antichrist and from the nations, to join with Him in His rule and reign in Israel.

In Matthew 24 we read, "When ye therefore shall see the abomination of desolation, spoken of by Daniel the prophet, stand in the holy place." The "holy place" is in Jerusalem. Daniel is a Jewish prophet writing to the Jewish people concerning their future. He cautioned his people to pray that their flight be not in winter or on the Sabbath day. The Jewish law restricts travel on the Sabbath, so if they are to obey the Mosaic law, they could not travel more than a mile. Thus, the caution to pray that their flight from Jerusalem be not on the Sabbath.

The troubles that begin at the beginning of the week of

years and extend to the end of the week are called the
"birth pangs of the nation of Israel." When the Bible speaks
of these tribulations the word that is used is the Greek word
odino, and it refers to the agonies of Israel under the antichrist, just before she becomes nationally the elect and chosen
people of the Lord Himself, over which He will rule and
reign in Jerusalem.

The Bible teaches us that the nation will travail as in birth
pangs. It will travail until it is delivered by Christ at His return
to the earth. In Zechariah 12:10 we read,

> And I will pour upon the house of David, and upon the in-
> habitants of Jerusalem, the spirit of grace and of supplications:
> and they shall look upon me whom they have pierced, and they
> shall mourn for him, as one mourneth for his only son, and shall
> be in bitterness for him, as one that is in bitterness for his first-
> born.

Christ is the One whom they have pierced. In the fourteenth
chapter of Zechariah there is a tremendous account of the
events that are going to take place in that day, when the
Lord comes and gathers all nations against Jerusalem to
battle.

> Behold, the day of the Lord cometh, and thy spoil shall be
> divided in the midst of thee.
> For I will gather all nations against Jerusalem to battle; and
> the city shall be taken, and the houses rifled, and the women
> ravished; and half of the city shall go forth into captivity, and
> the residue of the people shall not be cut off from the city.
> Then shall the Lord go forth, and fight against those nations,
> as when he fought in the day of battle.
> And his feet shall stand in that day upon the Mount of
> Olives, which is before Jerusalem on the east, and the Mount of
> Olives shall cleave in the midst thereof toward the east and
> toward the west, and there shall be a very great valley; and half
> of the mountain shall remove toward the north, and half of it
> toward the south.
> And ye shall flee to the valley of the mountains; for the valley

of the mountains shall reach unto Azal: yea, ye shall flee, like as ye fled from before the earthquake in the days of Uzziah king of Judah: and the Lord my God shall come, and all the saints with thee.

And it shall come to pass in that day, that the light shall not be clear, nor dark:

But it shall be one day which shall be known to the Lord, not day, nor night: but it shall come to pass, that at evening time it shall be light.

And it shall be in that day, that living waters shall go out from Jerusalem; half of them toward the former sea, and half of them toward the hinder sea in summer and in winter shall it be.

And the Lord shall be king over all the earth: in that day shall there be one Lord, and his name one.

All the land shall be burned as a plain from Geba to Rimmon south of Jerusalem: and it shall be lifted up, and inhabited in her place, from Benjamin's gate unto the place of the first gate, unto the corner gate, and from the tower of Hananeel unto the king's winepresses.

And men shall dwell in it, and there shall be no more utter destruction; but Jerusalem shall be safely inhabited.

And this shall be the plague wherewith the Lord will smite all the people that have fought against Jerusalem: Their flesh shall consume away while they stand upon their feet, and their eyes shall consume away in their holes, and their tongue shall consume away in their mouth.

And it shall come to pass in that day, that a great tumult from the Lord shall be among them; and they shall lay hold every one on the hand of his neighbour, and his hand shall rise up against the hand of his neighbour.

And Judah also shall fight at Jerusalem; and the wealth of all the heathen round about shall be gathered together, gold, and silver, and apparel, in great abundance.

And so shall be the plague of the horse, of the mule, of the camel, and of the ass, and of all the beasts that shall be in these tents, as this plague.

And it shall come to pass, that every one that is left of all the nations which came against Jerusalem shall even go up from year to year to worship the King, the Lord of Hosts, and to keep the feast of tabernacles.

And it shall be, that whoso will not come up of all the families of the earth unto Jerusalem to worship the King, the Lord of hosts, even upon them shall be no rain.

And if the family of Egypt go not up, and come not, they have no rain; there shall be the plague, wherewith the Lord will smite the heathen that come not up to keep the feast of tabernacles. This shall be the punishment of Egypt, and the punishment of all nations that come not up to keep the feast of tabernacles.

In that day shall there be upon the bells of the horses, HOLINESS UNTO THE LORD: and the pots in the Lord's house shall be like the bowls before the altar.

Yea, every pot in Jerusalem and in Judah shall be holiness unto the Lord of hosts: and all they that sacrifice shall come and take of them, and see the therein: and in that day there shall be no more of the Canaanite in the house of the Lord of Hosts.

Zechariah has said the city shall be taken, the houses rifled, the women ravished, and half the city shall go forth into captivity, and the rest of the people shall not be cut off from the city. "Then," he says, "shall the Lord go forth and fight against these nations as when he fought in the day of battle." This is an account of the battle that will occur at this time, when the enemies of the Lord are destroyed, and the remnant of the Jewish people that are left are brought forth once more, as the nation that God selected many centuries ago (Matthew 24:31).

The travail of Israel to live as a nation in the family of nations will begin before the antichrist comes. Israel became a nation in 1948, and already she has suffered many problems. She is going to suffer many more. When Jesus said that all of these signs will come to pass in this generation, He was not speaking of the generation alive then. He was speaking of the generation that would be in existence when these signs begin to come to pass, and this generation living then, would see *all* of these signs at one time, just as the generation of Noah suffered all of the tragedy of the flood.

When Jesus said that the gospel of the kingdom would be preached as a witness to all nations before the end comes, He was speaking about the kingdom that John the Baptist preached about: the kingdom of the Messiah that the Jews were looking for and that they still expect. This kingdom, they believed, would be the golden age of earth.

This same gospel of the kingdom, which is purely Jewish, will be preached again, from the time of the setting up of the abomination of desolation, to all of the world. In the book of Revelation, we see how this is going to be accomplished. John says that an angel, a messenger, will go forth into all of the world preaching the gospel of the kingdom during this week of years.

The abomination of desolation concerns only the temple in Jerusalem and the nation of Israel. The fleeing of the Jews from Judea at the time of the setting up of the abomination proves that only Israel is involved.

The *great tribulation,* from the setting up of the abomination, according to the book of Revelation and according to Jesus, concerns only the nation of Israel. The "elect" spoken of in the twenty-fourth chapter of Matthew (verses 21 through 26) whom Christ will fully regather when He comes again, as we have read about in the Old Testament, are the Jews. Jesus will gather them from the four corners of the earth, and from this secret place where they have been scattered, and protected, and bring them back again, purging out the rebels before He sets up His kingdom (Matthew 24:31).

The judgment of the nations at the return of Christ to earth, which we read about in the twenty-fifth chapter of Matthew (called the sheep and goat judgment) is based entirely upon how the nations treated the Jews. The context of Matthew 25 proves that as the basis of this judgment.

Many people believe that the judgment of the nations, where people are separated as sheep and goats, applies to individuals in the Church Age. This is not true. In that judgment there is no resurrection. In the sheep and goat judgment, there is no Book of Life. In the sheep and goat judgment, only the nations are judged, and the basis of judgment is not how they have read the Bible, or what they have done in the Church. Again, the basis of the sheep and goat judgment is how they have treated Jesus' brethren, the Jews—whether they have visited them when they were sick, or fed them when they were hungry, or clothed them when they were naked, or gave them drink when they were thirsty. They said, "Why, Lord, when did we see thee, or do this?" and He said, "In as much as you have done it to one of the least of these, my brethren, you have done it unto me."

Another reason we believe the sheep and goat judgment is related to the nations and their treatment of the Jews is based upon the fact that whether or not they are saved out of that judgment depends upon the works they have done or have not done. As we are saved by faith alone, we recognize that this is not the judgment for the Church. The Church cannot be substituted in any of the passages we have noted. The Church is raptured before these things occur. Lawlessness abounds on the earth because its hinderer, the Church, is in heaven. The antichrist then makes his appearance, and becomes a great power in the middle of the seven-year week, or the 1260 days, or the three and a half years, as it is spoken of in the book of Revelation.

These signs will be fulfilled in one generation, and that generation will be living at the time, or will begin somewhere around the time, that the nation of Israel is gathered the second time as a nation. The nation of Israel was sent into captivity in the Old Testament because of disobedience. They were allowed to return and rebuild the wall and temple of Jerusalem, and the seventy weeks of the prophecy of Daniel began to find their fulfillment in the time of their first regathering. Four hundred and eighty-three years of that four-hundred-and-ninety-year prophecy came to a conclusion at the time of the death of Jesus Christ. There are seven more years still unfulfilled.

Forty years after the death and resurrection of Jesus, the temple was destroyed and the Jews were dispersed in all of the nations of the Gentiles. Now they are regathering the second time as a nation. There is ample reason from prophecy and earthly signs to believe that the seventieth week of the prophecy of Daniel could begin its fulfillment soon. The Bible says these signs will be fulfilled in one generation. (A Biblical generation consists of about forty years.)

Daniel speaks in chapter 12 of the rapid increase of travel and the increase of knowledge. Less than fifty years ago the first automobiles had to travel on dirt roads. In those days the railway engines and the steamboats were tremendous ways of travel. It took a great number of days to go from one end of this country to the other. Travel abroad was especially slow.

Today jet planes make rapid travel from continent to continent a matter of just a few hours. Airplanes are getting bigger and faster. The Bible says, "Many will run to and fro." Our own nation is a nation on wheels, and the very economy of this nation depends upon all of us buying automobiles every two or three years, and spending most of our lives in them.

Regarding the increase of knowledge, the textbooks of five years ago concerning sciences, and the state of the universe, are already obsolete. Today's children, at the age of twelve, know more facts than their parents did at the age of twenty. There are improved methods of teaching that breed a rapid increase of knowledge. The only thing that I pray might go hand-in-hand with this increase of secular knowledge would be a rapid increase in the knowledge of the Word of God.

More than ten million of our young people will be in college, or are already in college, and, in the predicted future, three times that number will have college educations. The tragedy is that of all the benefits that go with this increase of knowledge, the increase in the quality of our cultural life and scientific knowledge, there is a marked decrease in the moral nature of man. The moral nature of man has not kept pace with the cultural increase. It seems that the more cultured men get, the farther away they are from God.

According to a Presidential Commission that investigated these facts, the increase in knowledge does not prevent crime. Statistics prove that the increase in crime that is in the world today has kept the same pace with the increase in knowledge. As a man gathers more of the wisdom of the world, and depends upon his own insight into the nature of things, he gets farther from God, the more inclined he is to live for himself and to be wicked.

The Bible speaks of great deceptions and delusions, and an abundance of false doctrines, the spirits of demons, and many other signs that are listed as signs of the end of the age in the Scriptures. These, in general, are lying, seared consciences, and forbidding to marry. It seems that marriage is becoming "old-fashioned" as more and more men and women are contented to just live together.

Men will become lovers of themselves, covetous, boasters, proud, blasphemers, disobedient to parents, unthankful, unholy, without natural affection. They will be trucebreakers, false accusers, incontinent (unrestrained in their passions and appetites), fierce, despisers of those that are good, traitors, heady, highminded, lovers of pleasures more than lovers of God.

The church of the Laodecians was accused of being lukewarm and naked just as the Church today is naked. Many people in the Church are not aware of their condition. The Bible speaks of increased labor troubles, in the times just preceding the end. James 5:1 and 8 speaks of a time of colossal riches and increased poverty, a time when men will want to rob one another of their wages or of their time. This prophecy is being fulfilled today.

There will be scoffers, mocking the doctrine of the coming of the Lord. If every member of the Church believed that the coming of the Lord was near, I believe they'd be faithful. This proves again the truth of the Word of God.

The second gathering of the nation of Israel is the prime point in the selection of the signs of the times. The first regathering of Israel was after the Babylonian captivity. She was scattered again in A.D. 70. Ezekiel, in his vision of the valley of dry bones, prophesied over those bones, and they shook, rattled, and stood up. He prophesied again, and flesh and sinew came upon them and they had life, and became a mighty army. This is prophetic of the regathering of Israel the second time.

The second regathering has been taking place since 1948. There are already over three million of the some ten million Jews in the world in Israel, and more and more are coming back every day. Of course, all of them will not go back until the second advent of Christ, because the Bible says that He will send His angels to the four corners of the earth and gather His elect. This is the *Jewish* elect. He will bring them back into Israel in order to purge them, but there are already enough people in Israel to constitute a nation in the eyes of the world.

Since Israel has been there twenty-eight years already as a nation, and since all of these signs will come to pass in the last generation of the age, and since a Bible generation is approximately forty years, we are certain that we are living in the evening of the Gentile age.

There are some general signs already in prospect—earthquakes and general famine in all the world—which have been predicted by the men who are in charge of famine control in the United Nations, to begin about 1976. These are men who are well versed in the science of agriculture and who know what this earth can bring forth, and who are comparing the means of production as over and against the population explosion, and saying that a famine of tremendous and drastic proportions will begin in 1976, and we will not be able to stop the death of uncounted millions of people. The shortage of oil from which fertilizer comes may cause this great shortage of agricultural products.

Since Israel has been a nation twenty-eight years, and already in birth pangs, it could be possible that the last week of years of the prophecy of Daniel may find the beginning of its fulfillment soon. These signs will come to pass in one Bible generation. It is the end of the age—the end of the Gentile age, which will bring the ushering in of the kingdom age, or the golden age, as the Jews spoke of it so many times in the Old Testament.

In the twenty-fourth and twenty-fifth chapters of Matthew we also have parables, and I want to refer briefly to the meanings of those. The parable of the fig tree in Matthew 24 is applied to the Jewish nation. Jesus said, "When the fig tree buds in the spring time, you know that summer is near." Often in Scripture Israel has been compared to a fig tree. If that is the way it is to be interpreted, the fig tree has already budded. The nation of Israel is a reality. Others will say that is not the meaning of the parable. It does mean, though, that summer is near when the fig tree buds, so you may know the second coming of Jesus is near when Israel is a nation in their land.

The second parable is the parable of the good man and his house. This parable teaches that the Jewish people are to be ready for the coming of Jesus Christ when they see these things coming to pass.

The next parable is the parable of the faithful and evil servants. This parable means that the Jewish people ought to be faithful, in view of these things coming to pass.

The next parable is of the ten virgins. Many people have used the parable of the ten virgins to mean the rapture of the church, but it could not mean this because this is a Jewish parable. Jesus is speaking of an event that happened often in Jerusalem, and when He used the marriage, the coming of the bridegroom, and the virgins being prepared and unprepared, it speaks of the virgins having a time to get up and trim their lamps to go and meet the bridegroom. The Bible teaches for the Church age that when the rapture comes it will be so quick we will not have time to trim our lamps. We will go in a moment, in the twinkling of an eye. There will be no trimming of the lamps for Church members because of the suddenness of the rapture.

The parable of the ten virgins applies to the Jewish people during the tribulation. When they see these things listed in Matthew 24 and 25 coming to pass, they are to be looking and waiting for the bridegroom and the party (the raptured Church) to come, so that they can be ready. If they are not ready, they will not be allowed in to the Kingdom, or the wedding feast. They will be shut out of the Kingdom age.

The rapture will have already taken place as far as the parable of the virgins is concerned. The parable of the virgins is a Jewish parable, and it refers to the Jews who are waiting and who know that Jesus is on His way, and who realize that He is coming. They are to have their lamps already trimmed and ready. It has nothing to do with the Church.

We know this is the true interpretation because of the connection with the rest of the chapter. Jesus says, "Then [at the literal coming of Christ to the earth] shall the kingdom of heaven be likened unto ten virgins. . . . Watch ye therefore for ye know neither the day nor the hour wherein the Son of man cometh to earth."

The parable of the judgment of the nations follows that immediately. Since the parables of the virgins and the talents indicate that Jesus is coming, the parable of the judgment of the nations follows because Jesus *has* come. He gathers before Him all of the nations of the earth, and He separates them as a shepherd would divide his flock—the sheep are set on the right hand and the goats are set on the left hand—and the sheep that are set on the right hand will be those accounted worthy to enter the millennial kingdom and to live in the golden age of the earth until the end of the kingdom age. Those that are called goats in this judgment will be turned into hell.

The judgment of the living nations is not a judgment of Christians. The judgment of the Christians has already taken place after the rapture of the Church in Heaven at the Judgment Seat of Christ. The judgment of the nations is a judgment on the earth. It has to do with the Gentile nations, as to the way they have treated the Jews, God's chosen and elect people.

When you read Matthew 24 and 25, remember that Jesus is speaking to the Jews, concerning the last week of the prophecy of Daniel, much of which is described in Revelation, chapters 6 through 19. It has to do with the time of Jacob's trouble, prophesied in the Old Testament. It has to do with the purging out of the rebels and the God-haters among the Jews, and the sending away into hell of the nations of the world who persecuted the Jews. The judgment of the living nations has nothing at all to do with the Church. Every word, every sign, every symbol, every admonition is Jewish in origin, and Jewish in intent.

I do believe that this is the proper exposition of Matthew 24 and 25 concerning the signs of the end, when Jesus will come visibly to the earth. Many of these signs are already present in an increased way in the world, such as increase of knowledge, the increase of travel, wars, famine, and pestilence.

Israel is already in the land as a nation. Because these signs apply to the Jewish people and not to the Church, we do not want to imply that there is any time for us to be lax. Because these signs are already tremendously increased, we cannot help but believe that the rapture of the Church could happen any time.

The reason that I want you to be concerned about this is not that you might be frightened, or that you might think you have plenty of time, or that it does not matter what you do. God has called us to be His representatives. John says this speaking of the second coming of Christ for the Church:

Behold, what manner of love the Father has bestowed upon us that we should be called the sons of God. Therefore the world knoweth us not because it knew Him not. Beloved, now are we the sons of God and it doth not appear yet what we shall be but we know that when He shall appear, we shall be like Him for we shall see Him as He is. And every man that hath this hope in him, purifieth himself even as He is pure. (I John 2:1-3)

The hope of the second coming of Christ, the hope of His coming in glory for the Church, and the second coming in visible appearance to judge the nations and to set up His reign in Israel is a hope that is a purifying hope. Any man, woman, boy, or girl of responsible age who can believe that Jesus Christ can come for the Church any moment, if they are honest and sincere about going to be with the Lord, will prepare and try to be a better person.

They will not be "bad-mouthing" their neighbors or their husbands, or their wives, or their brothers in Christ. They are not going to be cheating a man of his wages; or cheating a man of the work they do for their own wages. They are not going to be downriding and backbiting everybody else in the world. They are going to want to be more like Jesus, if they think they may be face to face with Him in the next moment. I believe with all my heart this is exactly why Paul and John have inserted this doctrine in the New Testament. It is so that we might be alerted and alarmed and ready for the instantaneous removal, or the snatching away, the catching up of the Church of Jesus Christ, to be forever with the Lord in the air.

IV

The Millennial Kingdom

In this chapter we will be studying from the twentieth chapter of the book of Revelation concerning the millennial reign of Christ. Please note that Revelation chapter 20 begins immediately following the coming of Christ, and His bringing death and destruction on the antichrist and his armies, at the end of the seven-year period called Daniel's seventieth week of prophecy. The judgment of the nations studied in Matthew 25 follows the battle of Armageddon. The setting up of the twelve restored tribes of Israel in that portion of the earth that God had promised them in Abraham will follow immediately. We shall begin our study following the great events of chapter 19. Read Revelation chapter 19:19-21 and chapter 20:1-7:

And I saw the beast, and the kings of the earth, and their armies, gathered together to make war against him that sat on the horse, and against his army.

And the beast was taken, and with him the false prophet that wrought miracles before him, with which he deceived them that had received the mark of the beast, and them that worshipped his image. These both were cast alive into a lake of fire burning with brimstone.

And the remnant were slain with the sword of him that sat upon the horse, which sword proceeded out of his mouth: and all the fowls were filled with their flesh.

* * *

And I saw an angel come down from heaven, having the key of the bottomless pit and a great chain in his hand.

And he laid hold on the dragon, that old serpent, which is the Devil, and Satan, and bound him a thousand years,

And cast him into the bottomless pit, and shut him up, and

set a seal upon him, that he should deceive the nations no more, till the thousand years should be fulfilled: and after that he must be loosed a little season.

And I saw thrones, and they sat upon them, and judgment was given unto them: and I saw the souls of them that were beheaded for the witness of Jesus, and for the word of God, and which had not worshipped the beast, neither his image, neither had received his mark upon their foreheads, or in their hands; and they lived and reigned with Christ a thousand years.

But the rest of the dead lived not again until the thousand years were finished. This is the first resurrection.

Blessed and holy is he that hath part in the first resurrection: on such the second death hath no power, but they shall be priests of God and of Christ, and shall reign with him a thousand years.

And when the thousand years are expired, Satan shall be loosed out of his prison.

Every time I teach about this thousand-year reign there are many wonderful, well-meaning people, who indicate that they believe that this is all symbolical, or that it should be spiritualized; but I fail to see how we can spiritualize any of this Scripture because of the literal sense of the Word. We know that the antichrist and his armies will be destroyed. They are real people. We know that Jesus will come with all of the saints. They, also, are real. We know that the Bible says that the rest of the dead live not again until the thousand years were finished. These years are literal years, and the people are real people.

"Blessed and holy is he that hath part in the first resurrection"—this is a real group of people. The Bible speaks of binding Satan in a real prison with a real chain. How can you bind a spirit with a literal chain? We know that it is possible for the angels in any dispensation to assume bodily form, and certainly it is not impossible for Satan to assume a bodily form. Jesus said to His disciples (in His resurrection body), "Handle me and see. Touch me." He could eat or drink as He chose. He could appear and disappear as He chose.

Nevertheless, He was a visible, real person when the occasion demanded it.

I fail to see, since this time of the age is attended with the death and destruction of the wicked antichrist and his armies, and with the resurrection of the righteous dead at the beginning of the millennium, and is ended with the resurrection of the wicked dead at the ending of the millennium, how we can spiritualize these literal truths away and say that this does not mean that Jesus is going to reign a thousand years.

How many times does the word *thousand* find itself in this Scripture? It is found six times. How often does the Lord have to say anything to us to make us believe what He says? If He said it only one time, I would believe it. We see here in this Scripture a literal time that will come at the end of this age, and this end of the age is the end of the times of the Gentiles. This is what Jesus had reference to when He gave the Great Commission to the Church, "Go out into all of the world and preach the gospel to every creature and lo, I am with you always, even unto the end of the 'eon' [or the 'age']," or as some people have translated it, the "world." The present world *kosmos*, the present society, is the literal meaning of the word *eon*. When the end of the Gentile age arrives, there comes the age of the visible reign of Christ on the earth with His saints, who have been resurrected from the dead, and who have been caught up prior to the tribulation week, and as He comes visibly to gather back to Palestine the people of Israel.

The definition of this dispensation is so called the millennial reign of Christ, not because the word *millennium* is in the Bible, but because the word *millennium* is Latin for a thousand years. It is a dispensation of time when God, along with the Son and the Holy Spirit, sets up the visible reign of Christ on the earth, and this divine government will begin then to reign over the nations of the earth forever.

In the twentieth chapter of the book of Revelation it is

called "the thousand year reign of Christ." It is called in Ephesians 1:10 "the dispensation of the fulness of time." The Bible speaks of it in the book of Acts, in chapter 3, verses 19-21, as "the times of restitution of all things; when the seasons of refreshing of the earth will come." This is referring to the millennial reign of Christ.

Please note what the following Scriptures have to say about the millennium:

> For the day of the Lord of hosts shall be upon every one that is proud and lofty, and upon every one that is lifted up; and he shall be brought low. (Isaiah 2:12)

> For the day is near, even the day of the Lord is near, a cloudy day; it shall be the time of the heathen. (Ezekiel 30:3)

> Woe unto you that desire the day of the Lord! to what end is it for you? the day of the Lord is darkness, and not light. (Amos 5:18)

> Blow ye the trumpet in Zion, and sound an alarm in my holy mountain: let all the inhabitants of the land tremble: for the day of the Lord cometh, for it is nigh at hand; (Joel 2:1)

> Behold, the day of the Lord cometh, and thy spoil shall be divided in the midst of thee. (Zechariah 14:1)

> Hold thy peace at the presence of the Lord God: for the day of the Lord is at hand: for the Lord hath prepared a sacrifice, he hath bid his guests. (Zephaniah 1:7)

> For, behold, the day cometh, that shall burn as an oven; and all the proud, yea, and all that do wickedly, shall be stubble: and the day that cometh shall burn them up, saith the Lord of hosts, that it shall leave them neither root nor branch. (Malachi 4:1)

> But of the times and the seasons, brethren, ye have no need that I write unto you.

> For yourselves know perfectly that the day of the Lord so cometh as a thief in the night. (I Thessalonians 5:1-2)

> Now we beseech you, brethren, by the coming of our Lord Jesus Christ, and by our gathering together unto him,
> That ye be not soon shaken in mind, or be troubled, neither by spirit, nor by word, nor by letter as from us, as that the day of Christ is at hand. (II Thessalonians 2:1-2)

> But the day of the Lord will come as a thief in the night; in the which the heavens shall pass away with a great noise, and the elements shall melt with fervent heat, the earth also and the works that are therein shall be burned up. (II Peter 3:10)

In all of the above Scriptures, the millennial reign of Christ is referred to as "the day of the Lord."

It is referred to in Matthew 12:32 as "the world to come."

> And whosoever speaketh a word against the Son of man, it shall be forgiven him: but whosoever speaketh against the Holy Ghost, it shall not be forgiven him, neither in this world, neither in the world to come.

In the world to come, or in the age to come, Jesus said that many would sit down with Him in the kingdom. That is the age to come, "the millennium," that He was speaking of.

It is spoken of as "the kingdom of Christ and God" in the following Scriptures:

> For this ye know, that no whoremonger, nor unclean person, nor covetous man, who is an idolater, hath any inheritance in the kingdom of Christ and of God. (Ephesians 5:5)

> I charge thee therefore before God, and the Lord Jesus Christ, who shall judge the quick and the dead at his appearing and his kingdom; (II Timothy 4:1)

> To deliver such an one unto Satan for the destruction of the flesh, that the spirit may be saved in the day of the Lord Jesus. (I Corinthians 5:5)

I beheld, and the same horn made war with the saints, and
prevailed against them;
    Until the Ancient of days came, and judgment was given to
the saints of the most High; and the time came that the saints
possessed the kingdom. (Daniel 7:21-22)

In the fourteenth chapter of the book of Mark it is called the
"kingdom of God" and "the times of restoration of all things"
in Acts 3. It is called "the consolation of Israel" in the Old
Testament. For example, this is what Simeon was looking for
when Mary brought Jesus to the Temple. The consolation of
Israel means the redemption of Jerusalem.

Why would it be called this? Why will Israel be consoled
in this age? This is because they are going to be restored to
divine favor with God: that is, those that are left on earth
following the great tribulation period. Because of Messiah's
presence they will become the head of the nations, and no
longer the least. This is called in the Bible "the consolation of
Israel."

In Luke 1:32 Gabriel made this promise to Mary:

He shall be great, and shall be called the Son of the Highest:
and the Lord God shall give unto him the throne of his father
David.

That promise has never been fulfilled to this day. Some will
say that Jesus is now reigning on the throne of His father
David. There is no book, chapter, or verse in Scripture that
teaches this. The Scriptures do teach, however, that Jesus is
presently on the right hand of God the Father. He has not
reigned over the house of Israel forever because Israel has
rejected Him as their king. He will not reign over the house
of Israel forever until Israel accepts Him as their Messiah,
when the nation is born in one day, and when a fountain is
opened for their cleansing in one day, and in one day the
spirit of repentance and regeneration will be given to them
by God Himself, when Jesus appears the second time, visibly,

to take up and begin His reign on the earth. The millennial age will end with the great white throne judgment and the casting of Satan and his armies into the lake of fire forever. He will never be released again after that.

The Old Testament foretells this kingdom. All during the age of the captivity of the Israelites, when the prophets were writing concerning God's hope for them, this kingdom was foretold. God made covenants with Abraham, and with David. God guaranteed to Abraham and to David, in the Old Testament, an everlasting earthly kingdom, and the Bible says that God is not a man that He should lie.

There are those that say that the word *everlasting* does not mean lasting forever. But then, what does it mean? If God said to you, "I am going to give you an everlasting kingdom," would you not believe that it would be everlasting? Lasting forever? God promised Israel this, but when Israel was divided into two kingdoms, in the year 1009 B.C., it did not look as though it was coming to pass. A little later they went into captivity. In their captivity, God raised up prophets to emphasize to Israel that He would still keep His promises to them, if they would obey Him. If they would return to Him, and if they would stop rebelling against Him, and if they would fulfill His righteous requirements, He promised to fulfill His Word. Sixteen prophets wrote concerning these promises. Did these prophets lie? No. Have these promises ever been fulfilled? No.

If we are to believe the words of God's own prophets, then it must come to pass. There is a time coming when these passages will be fulfilled. Because of the rebellion of Israel, these prophets wrote that they were going to go into captivity, which they did, and that they would be scattered among the nations. They were scattered among the nations according to these prophecies, and the Bible says that they would be many days without a king, a sacrifice, or a knowledge of the true God, and that after this, they would be gathered back to their

own land, and be brought very low, because of the oppression
of the Gentiles. *Then* they would be delivered from the nations
by the coming of the Messiah.

Israel is presently in the second earthly regathering, and
they are showing signs of strength. According to the Bible,
they will be brought very low before they believe in Jesus
as their Messiah.

Here are the Scripture references to this for you to look up:
Isaiah 1:2-9, Isaiah 7:12-13, Isaiah 63:1-6, Jeremiah 33:17,
Ezekiel 24:11, Daniel 7:12-27, Hosea 2:14, Hebrews 11, Joel
2:28, Micah 4:1-14, Zechariah 8:1-14, Malachi 3:1-4, II Samuel
7, Luke 1:30-35, Luke 21:20-24, Acts 15:13-17, Romans 11:25-27,
Revelation 1:5, Revelation 5:10, Mark 15:43 and Acts 3:19-21.

The millennial kingdom will begin when the Lord Jesus
Christ returns in glory.

> When the Son of man shall come in his glory, and all the
> holy angels with him, then shall he sit upon the throne of his
> glory:
> And before him shall be gathered all nations: and he shall
> separate them one from another, as a shepherd divideth his
> sheep from the goats:
> And he shall set the sheep on his right hand, but the goats on
> the left.
> Then shall the King say unto them on his right hand, Come,
> ye blessed of my Father, inherit the kingdom prepared for you
> from the foundation of the world:
> For I was an hungred, and ye gave me meat: I was thirsty,
> and ye gave me drink: I was a stranger, and ye took me in:
> Naked, and ye clothed me: I was sick, and ye visited me: I
> was in prison, and ye came unto me.
> Then shall the righteous answer him, saying, Lord, when
> saw we thee an hungred, and fed thee? or thirsty, and gave thee
> drink?
> When saw we thee a stranger, and took thee in? or naked,
> and clothed thee?
> Or when saw we thee sick, or in prison, and came unto thee?
> And the King shall answer and say unto them, Verily I say
> unto you, Inasmuch as ye have done it unto one of the least of
> these my brethren, ye have done it unto me.

Then shall he say also unto them on the left hand, Depart from me, ye cursed, into everlasting fire, prepared for the devil and his angels:

For I was an hungred, and ye gave me no meat: I was thirsty, and ye gave me no drink:

I was a stranger, and ye took me not in: naked, and ye clothed me not: sick, and in prison, and ye visited me not.

Then shall they also answer him, saying, Lord, when saw we thee an hungred, or athirst, or a stranger, or naked, or sick, or in prison, and did not minister unto thee?

Then shall he answer them, saying, Verily I say unto you, Inasmuch as ye did it not to one of the least of these, ye did it not to me.

And these shall go away into everlasting punishment: but the righteous into life eternal. (Matthew 25:31-46)

And I saw heaven opened, and behold a white horse; and he that sat upon him was called Faithful and True, and in righteousness he doth judge and make war.

His eyes were as a flame of fire, and on his head were many crowns; and he had a name written, that no man knew, but he himself.

And he was clothed with a vesture dipped in blood: and his name is called the Word of God.

And the armies which were in heaven followed him upon white horses, clothed in fine linen, white and clean.

And out of his mouth goeth a sharp sword, that with it he should smite the nations: and he shall rule them with a rod of iron: and he treadeth the winepress of the fierceness and wrath of Almighty God.

And he hath on his vesture and on his thigh a name written, KING OF KINGS, AND LORD OF LORDS.

And I saw an angel standing in the sun; and he cried with a loud voice, saying to all the fowls that fly in the midst of heaven, Come and gather yourselves together unto the supper of the great God;

That ye may eat the flesh of kings, and the flesh of captains, and the flesh of mighty men, and the flesh of horses, and of them that sit on them, and the flesh of all men, both free and bond, both small and great.

And I saw the beast, and the kings of the earth, and their armies, gathered together to make war against him that sat on the horse, and against his army.

And the beast was taken, and with him the false prophet that wrought miracles before him, with which he deceived them that had received the mark of the beast, and them that worshipped his image. These both were cast alive into a lake of fire burning with brimstone. (Revelation 19:11-20)

This Kingdom will be set up after the Church is raptured:

Behold, I shew you a mystery; We shall not all sleep, but we shall all be changed,

In a moment, in the twinkling of an eye, at the last trump: for the trumpet shall sound, and the dead shall be raised incorruptible, and we shall be changed.

For this corruptible must put on incorruption, and this mortal must put on immortality.

So when this corruptible shall have put on incorruption, and this mortal shall have put on immortality, then shall be brought to pass the saying that is written, Death is swallowed up in victory.

O death, where is thy sting? O grave, where is thy victory?

The sting of death is sin; and the strength of sin is the law.

But thanks be to God, which giveth us the victory through our Lord Jesus Christ.

Therefore, my beloved brethren, be ye steadfast, unmoveable, always abounding in the work of the Lord, forasmuch as ye know that your labour is not in vain in the Lord. (I Corinthians 15:51-58)

But I would not have you to be ignorant, brethren, concerning them which are asleep, that ye sorrow not, even as others which have no hope.

For if we believe that Jesus died and rose again, even so them also which sleep in Jesus will God bring with him.

For this we say unto you by the word of the Lord, that we which are alive and remain unto the coming of the Lord shall not prevent them which are asleep.

For the Lord himself shall descend from heaven with a shout, with the voice of the archangel, and with the trump of God: and the dead in Christ shall rise first:

Then we which are alive and remain shall be caught up together with them in the clouds to meet the Lord in the air: and so shall we ever be with the Lord. (I Thessalonians 4:13-17)

This kingdom will be set up after the future tribulation. It will begin after the seventieth week of the prophecy of Daniel has been fulfilled. Christ does not come back visibly with His saints to the earth until the fulfillment of the time of Jacob's trouble, or the tribulation period, is over.

The millennial kingdom will begin after Israel is gathered back from all countries. I want you to note when you search all of these Scriptures, concerning the time when Jesus comes back, certain events will take place. First of all, Christ draws all of the tribes of Israel from all over the world back to Israel, and He judges them. Then He judges the Gentile nations as to what they have done with His people and He purges them. Following this, the temple of Ezekiel is built. Then the reign of Christ will be set up in Jerusalem, in Ezekiel's Temple. Ezekiel's Temple will be built immediately after the restoration of all of the Israelite tribes as the restored nation, under the rulership of Christ, at the end of the week of tribulation, or the last seven years of Daniel's prophecy.

The Bible says that the kingdom of Christ is *after* all of these events. Yet many people would say that the kingdom of Christ is now. The Apostles themselves taught that the kingdom was future, at the second coming of Christ.

When Jesus ascended into Heaven some of the disciples with whom He had been for forty days, teaching them concerning the kingdom, said, "Wilt thou at this time restore the kingdom to Israel?" Jesus answered, "It is not for you to know the times or the seasons that the Father hath in His power." Jesus did not deny that the kingdom was going to be restored to Israel. In fact, He rather indicated that it would be, but that it would be in God's own time. If we had no other Scriptures for the future kingdom but that one, it would be sufficient, but there are others. In I Timothy 6:14-15 we find these words:

> That thou keep this commandment without spot, unrebukeable, until the appearing of our Lord Jesus Christ:
> Which in his times he shall shew, who is the blessed and only Potentate, the King of kings, and Lord of lords;

When Jesus appears visibly the second time, He will show to the nations of the earth, and to the nation of Israel, who is the King of kings, and certainly the kingdom will not be visibly present unless the King is visibly present.

This kingdom is going to be a literal and earthly kingdom just like any other literal and earthly kingdom. It will be the ninth kingdom in the process of the age of the earth, in connection with the nation of Israel. For example, in chapter 1 I said that Egypt was the first kingdom that persecuted the Jews. Following Egypt, Assyria was the second, Babylon was the third, the Medo-Persian kingdom was the fourth, Greece was the fifth, and Rome was the sixth. Then following the rapture of the Church, the setting up of the ten-nation federation in Europe will be the seventh (the revived Roman empire). The rupture of four of those kingdoms by the antichrist, and the setting up of his own dictatorship will be the eighth (this will be the old Grecian empire revived). When Jesus comes to rule and reign—this will be the ninth and last kingdom on this present earth.

What will be the form of government in this kingdom? In the kingdom age there will be a government conducted by the King, Jesus. There will be laws—they will be His. If there is government and law, there must be commerce; there must be industry. There is going to be a great deal of life as it is expressed right now. It will be a renewed life because of the renewed condition of the earth.

Since there will be laws and government, there will be schools. We will still have need to learn in that age. The teachings of the Lord will not be outlawed in those schools. In fact, the primary teaching in those schools will be the law of the Lord and what respects the age of the kingdom and the bringing in of the reign of universal righteousness.

All of the saints will already have been judged and rewarded at the judgment seat of Christ, according to the deeds done in their bodies. They will rule and reign with Christ in governmental exercise of authority in the millennial kingdom.

I want you to understand me when I make this next statement. One of the blessed privileges of being a member of the body of Christ is this: when Jesus comes for the Church, we will be changed in a moment, in the twinkling of an eye. We will receive our glorified spiritual bodies. The rest of the people left on the earth will not. This promise is for the Church. We will be in that glorified spiritual body from that moment on, throughout eternity, for whatever God has in store for us in the ages upon ages to come.

The people who live through the tribulation period and who are spared in the judgment of the nations will enter into the millennial reign, with the remnant of the Jews, and they will be natural earthly people. This is why we urge people to accept Christ during the age of the Church. Those who accept Christ in the age of the Church will have spirit bodies like Jesus throughout all of the ages of eternity; and the others who do not accept Him before the advent of the kingdom age, will live on the earth as a natural earthly person, if they are fortunate enough to get through the judgment of the nations, or the sheep and goat judgment.

While these natural people are living on the earth, life will be lengthened. The Bible says that the life of a man will be as the life of a tree during the millennial age, and the earth will bring forth plentifully, so much so that the ploughman will overtake the reapers. This means that they will hardly get the reaping of one harvest finished before the ploughman will be coming along saying, "Hurry. I must plant again." In the millennium, a person who dies at the age of ninety will be considered a child. In that age, the Scriptures say the lion will lie down with the lamb, and there will be no enmity between man and beast. "A little child will play on the hold of an asp, and the den of an adder, and nothing shall hurt or harm in all of my holy mountain." That is what the Scripture says about the Golden Age. Men will multiply and the word of the Lord will go forth from Jerusalem, and all of the other nations, seeing the blessings of God brought upon the Israelite nation, will say, "We want to serve Jesus." The nations are not doing that today.

During the millennial age, the Israelites will become God's great evangelists. This will be because of their ability to learn languages; because of their ability, as they've proven in the age of the Gentiles, to go into any country and settle and learn the customs and the language of that country, and yet maintain their separate identity. They will be the ambassadors of God, going into all the Gentile nations of the world during the millennial age preaching the wonderful riches of the kingdom gospel of the Lord Jesus Christ.

In the millennial age, all of the world will hear about Jesus. The Bible says that everyone shall know the Lord, from the least to the greatest, and no man will have to say another will teach him, because all will know Him by reason of the knowledge that goes forth through the evangelistic work of the nation of Israel.

Does this give a "second chance"? No, it does not. Back during the age of the Old Testament, people had one chance to be right with God. They could believe the law of Moses and die in faith in the coming of the Messiah and be saved, or they could reject it. There is no second chance for them.

If people will not believe the Lord in the New Testament age, and die in unbelief, they are lost eternally. There is no second chance. Anyone who is lost in any age, will be in the realm of the wicked dead, and they will be there until the end of the thousand years, when they are raised for the judgment of the great white throne.

In the week of the tribulation period, the last seven years of this present age, those people who are living then will still either believe on Christ or be lost. During the millennial age, people will either believe on and obey the words of Christ, or they will be lost. There is no other way—there is no second chance for anyone.

However, all these things will not affect the Church because the Church will be ruling and reigning in the millennial age forever, as spiritual co-inheritors with Jesus Christ. This has been the plan of God for the sons of God adopted from the families of the earth. If I could convince every member of the Church that this is God's plan for His children, and that we are to be spirit people with Jesus—visible, even as Jesus will be visible—but spirit people, ruling and reigning with Him as priests in the coming kingdom, throughout the eternal ages to come, bringing His knowledge and will and life and abundant living to all of the worlds of the universe, we would never have to have another attendance campaign or another revival meeting. We would never have to beg people to come to church. In fact, we would have to have people especially elected and appointed to baptize people in obedience to Christ, and to get them ready—if they really believed this.

Far too many are like Esau. Esau was the firstborn of Isaac, and had, by right of being the firstborn, all of the birthright that God had promised Abraham in His covenant with him. For what did he give up this birthright? The Bible says a mess of pottage. A dish of lentils and beans, or red soup. All of that wonderful birthright was given up because he was hungry. Today many members of the church are giving up all of what God has planned for us, as sons of God, for a mess of pottage—for earthly things, simply, the surfeiting, the eating and drinking and the cares of this world.

Some people will not be in this millennial kingdom. Jesus said in Matthew 5:20, "Except your righteousness exceed that of the scribes and the Pharisees, you shall in no wise enter in the kingdom of heaven." What about the righteousness of the scribes and Pharisees? They prayed, fasted, were strict observers of the letter of the law, they tithed. They did all of the outward things. They left undone, though, the weightier matters of law, justice, and mercy, and that is the element that Christ came to bring to the everyday practical life of the Christian. Yet, He said to those same people, "Except your righteousness exceed theirs, you will not enter into the kingdom."

In the tribulation period of time, no one who receives the mark of the beast, or the number of his name, will be allowed to enter into the kingdom. The person who has not been a worthy user of his talents, will not enter into the kingdom. The person who would attend the wedding feast of the lamb, or the Son, without the wedding garment provided by the Lord of the feast himself, will not enter in. These people will not be subjects in the kingdom. They will be turned into hell with all of the nations that have forgotten and have left God out of their lives. I thank God that He has provided for us in all things through the death of His Son Jesus Christ.

The millennial kingdom will be literal and earthly. There will be earthly people in the kingdom. Those people who are fortunate enough to be in the body of Christ, the Church, having been taken to be with Jesus, judged and appointed their place in the kingdom, will be ruling and reigning with Jesus when He rules and reigns in that outward kingdom of the Israelites. The nations of the world will probably be located about where they are today (those that are left of the nations). They will send emissaries to Jerusalem on certain feast days in this kingdom. They will observe the Feast of Tabernacles and certain other feasts, not as a means of redemption, but as a means of reminding the people of all that God has done to bring them to this age—just as we observe the Lord's Supper and practice Christian baptism. For the nation who will not send an emissary to do this, the Bible says, "Upon that nation there will no rain fall." What happens when there is no rain? There will be no harvest.

The Bible says there is going to be a literal river flowing out of Ezekiel's temple. This may come about, as a result of the last great earthquake, when Jesus comes. It will flow eastward and southward. It will run through Jerusalem and south of Jerusalem. The river will be divided, and half of the river will flow westward into the Mediterranean Sea, and half of it will flow eastward into the Dead Sea. The Dead Sea will be elevated by reason of that earthquake and the Mount of Olives being split in two, so that it will have an outlet into the Mediterranean for the first time in the history of the world. We find this in the forty-seventh chapter of the book of Ezekiel.

At this present study, there are no fish in the Dead Sea, but salt, potassium and billions of dollars worth of minerals. Perhaps this is why there is such a fuss over the land of Palestine. The nations of the earth need those minerals and oil of the Middle East to carry on their wars against one another. During the millennium, though, they will be able to go fishing in the Dead Sea, because there is going to be a multitude of fish there. They will fish all the way up the banks of the river into the Dead Sea and, for fishermen, it will be a fisherman's paradise.

There will be trees on both sides of that river in the millennial kingdom and the leaf of the trees will not fade. They will bring forth new fruit, according to their months, and the trees will be for the healing and preservation of the natural life of the nations.

There will be a priesthood in the temple, but not of the Levitical priesthood because they failed in their purpose. The priesthood will be taken from the sons of Zadok who were faithful to David, in the kingdom age he lived.

The Bible speaks of spiritual conditions in the millennium. Joel, chapter two, says the Spirit will be poured out on all flesh. In Acts 2:38, on the day of Pentecost, Peter said, "This is that which was spoken by the prophet Joel when he speaks of the day of the Lord."

Pentecost was the beginning of the last day of the Lord, but that prophecy of Joel was not fulfilled entirely because God's spirit was not poured out on all people on that day. There was an initial outpouring on the apostles on Pentecost, another outpouring upon the household of Cornelius about eight years later, and special miraculous fillings of the Spirit as were needed in the age of the Church, until the New Testament was completed, but the general outpouring upon all flesh is reserved until Jesus comes visibly the second time and the nation of Israel is restored in the land.

The Bible says there will be universal knowledge in that day. One of the problems of our age is the lack of the ability of people to read and to write and to know. Today there is a great deal of ignorance all over the world, even with the knowledge explosion that is upon us now. In Isaiah 11:9 it speaks of universal knowledge:

> They shall not hurt nor destroy in all my holy mountain: for the earth shall be full of the knowledge of the Lord, as the waters cover the sea.

In Zechariah 8:22-23 the Bible also speaks of universal knowledge:

> Yea, many people and strong nations shall come to seek the Lord of hosts in Jerusalem, and to pray before the Lord.
> Thus saith the Lord of hosts; in those days it shall come to pass, that ten men shall take hold out of all languages of the nations, even shall take hold of the skirt of him that is a Jew, saying, We will go with you: for we have heard that God is with you.

This will be so that all people can know the ways of God, whether they want to walk in them or not. Many will walk in God's ways, but some will not, in the millennial age. There will be isolated instances of death in the millennial kingdom. There will be instances where people will feign righteousness, and they will be discovered as to the true intent of their hearts when the devil is let out of the pit for a little season and go out, at the end of the age, to deceive the nations once more, and gather a mighty army that encompasses the city of Jerusalem round about.

If everyone in the millennial age is going to know about

the will of God and many of them walk in it, it will be a great change from today. Today there are in the world nearly three billion people, but there are only about 600 million professed Christians of all groups. But how many really born-again Christians are there in this 600 million? Only God knows— but the majority are not real Christians.

A great change will be present in the millennial age because the Jews will be missionaries of the gospel and priests of the law. They will take the gospel message and the will of the Lord to all people. There will be a universal religion. There are some trying to bring a universal religion about today by various and sundry means, but in Malachi 1:11 the prophet says, concerning the millennial age, "From the rising of the sun even to the going down of the same shall my name be great among the Gentiles and in every place, incense shall be offered unto my name and a pure offering, for my name shall be great among the heathen, saith the Lord of hosts." That has never happened in our time. It will happen in the millennial age.

In Isaiah, chapter four, we find that the glory of the Lord will be continually manifest in the millennial age:

> When the Lord shall have washed away the filth of the daughters of Zion, and shall have purged the blood of Jerusalem from the midst thereof by the spirit of judgment, and by the spirit of burning.
> And the Lord will create upon every dwelling place of mount Zion, and upon her assemblies, a cloud and smoke by day, and the shining of a flaming fire by night: for upon all the glory shall be a defence.
> And there shall be a tabernacle for a shadow in the daytime from the heat, and for a place of refuge, and for a covert from storm and from rain.

There are other things that will be in the millennium. Satan will be bound—thank God for that. There will be no tempter in that age, as the songwriter says, "Satan will be bound a thousand years, there'll be no tempter then, when the Lord Himself will come to earth again." There will be universal peace. The Bible says, "The nations of the world will beat their swords into plowshares."

My friend, just think of all the multiplied billions of dollars that are spent every year upon the armaments of the world, to take away from other nations of the world because of greed! When you loose all that money in the millennial age to take care of the things that man ought to be taking care of now, it will be a great time for the people on earth who will be living then. There will be no more race prejudices, and no more national ills. The Lord will not permit this. He will be authoritarian. He will be the ruler, and those who do not obey Him will be done away with very quickly, according to the Bible.

There will be no unemployment. People will not come by every year and say, "Let's give to the United Fund." It will not be needed. The method of taxation will probably be the tithe. That's God's appointed way of raising revenue in the Old and the New, and He has indicated no change in the millennial age. All of the money we now spend for selfish purposes, will be released for doing the things that God would have us do, to make this earth the kind of place on which people will want to live. There will be full justice for all. The crime waves will be a thing of the past. Everybody will get full justice, and get it immediately. The Bible says that even while we are crying out for the Lord, He will hear us before we ask and He will avenge speedily any crimes that happen on the earth.

The Bible says there will be an increase in light.

> Moreover the light of the moon shall be as the light of the sun, and the light of the sun shall be sevenfold, as the light of seven days, in the day that the Lord bindeth up the breach of his people, and healeth the stroke of their wound. (Isaiah 30:26)

> Violence shall no more be heard in thy land, wasting nor destruction within thy borders; but thou shalt call thy walls Salvation, and thy gates Praise.
> The sun shall be no more thy light by day; neither for bright-

ness shall the moon give light unto thee: but the Lord shall be unto thee an everlasting light, and thy God thy glory.

Thy sun shall no more go down; neither shall thy moon withdraw itself: for the Lord shall be thine everlasting light, and the days of thy mourning shall be ended.

Thy people also shall be all righteous: they shall inherit the land for ever, the branch of my planting, the work of my hands, that I may be glorified.

A little shall become a thousand, and a small one a strong nation: I the Lord will hasten it in his time. (Isaiah 60:18-22)

Isaiah's prophecy in chapter 60 extends on over into the new heavens and the new earth, but the kingdom age is just the beginning of it, with the sevenfold increase of the light of the sun and the light of the moon.

I have already mentioned the changes in the animal kingdom. The lion himself will have his stomach changed so he can eat grass or straw. He will not have to eat meat. The land will be restored. I have spoken of the ploughman overtaking the reapers; the desert blossoming as the rose.

All of these blessings are found in Isaiah. Love and righteousness will prevail. It should prevail now in the age of the Church, but I know of very few churches where it does. Does it prevail in your church? Is everybody in love one with another?

Well, you say, what's the purpose of all this? What is the purpose of waiting? Why not just bring it all to pass now? The purpose of God in the millennial dispensation is to test man under ideal conditions, and put down all rebellion and all enemies under the feet of Christ, who was rejected, when He came the first time. All of this is spoken of in the New Testament in I Corinthians 15: "Then cometh the end [the final end], when He shall have delivered up the kingdom to God [the millennial kingdom], even to the father; when he shall have put down all rule and authority." He will then be King of kings and Lord of lords. Every knee shall bow, every tongue shall confess, every nation shall render homage to the Lord.

He must reign, in this millennial age, until He hath put all
enemies under His feet, and the last enemy to be destroyed is
death.

Death will not be destroyed until the end of the millennial
age. In the twentieth chapter of Revelation there are two
things mentioned that are cast into hell: "Death and hades
shall give up the dead which are in them." Death is put down
under the feet of Christ, and from then on, from the Great
White Throne judgment into eternity, there will be no more
death. The Bible says, "For he hath put all things under his
feet and when all things shall be subdued unto him, then shall
the Son also himself be subject unto him that put all things
under him, that God may be all in all" (I Corinthians 15:28).

Another purpose of the millennial age is to fulfill the
covenants that God made with Abraham, as recorded in Genesis.
God also made a covenant with Isaac which is recorded in
Genesis 26, and with Jacob, in Genesis 28. God made a covenant
with David, as recorded in II Samuel. These covenants are
perpetual. They are not to be broken.

In the millennial age Christ will be avenged, and He and
His saints will be vindicated. They will be given their proper
sphere of rule in the world.

Still another purpose of the millennial age is to fulfill the
promise of God to restore the nation of Israel from among the
nations of the world—to deliver them up and to make them
the head of the nations forever.

> And it shall come to pass in that day, that the Lord shall set
> his hand again the second time to recover the remnant of his
> people, which shall be left, from Assyria, and from Egypt, and
> from Elam, and from Shinar, and from Hamath, and from the
> islands of the sea. (Isaiah 11:11)

> As I live, saith the Lord God, surely with a mighty hand,
> and with a stretched out arm, and with fury poured out, will I
> rule over you. (Ezekiel 20:33)

And it shall come to pass, if thou shalt hearken diligently unto the voice of the Lord thy God, to observe and to do all his commandments which I command thee this day, that the Lord thy God will set thee on high above all nations of the earth. (Deuteronomy 28:1)

In the millennial age the saints of all the ages will be exalted in some kingly or priestly capacity, according to the promises of God and according to their works. He will gather together in one all things in Christ and judge the nations in righteousness and restore the earth to its original owners. Who was the original owner of the earth? It was Adam. Who usurped it? Satan. Satan is the prince of power in the air, and he is the prince of this age, but the earth is going to be restored to its original owners, the new Adams that are in Jesus Christ.

I hope that this is enough evidence for you to believe that the Bible is true and there must be a kingdom age following the age of the Gentiles in this world, where Jesus will reign visibly with the Church, and that we might understand that as the Church reigns with Him, the members will have the same type of spiritual body that Jesus has. We will be with Him as rulers of the entire universe forever, in connection with this, reign with Christ after the end of the millennial age. Throughout eternity there will be natural generations of people upon the earth who believed on Him during the millennial age, and they will be the ones who will inherit the new heavens and the new earth, along with the redeemed church members.

V

The New Heavens and New Earth

I have pointed out that the first resurrection took place at the beginning of the last week of the prophecy of Daniel, and the rest of the wicked dead (since the righteous dead were all resurrected in the first resurrection) were not raised until the thousand years were finished. It is at this time, when the thousand years are finished, that we begin this chapter.

I want the reader to stop now and read Revelation 20:5 through 21:7.

I believe the Bible literally. I believe that God wrote the message, or caused men to write the message in a language that could be understood. I do not believe that He would give His word in such a mysterious and symbolic language that He would condemn men to an eternal hell simply because they were not able to understand it. I do not believe (unless the particular context calls for it) that we ought to spiritualize and mysticize certain truths of God that we claim not to understand, or that we might say that we do not know what it means.

In our reading at this time, we read of the end of the thousand-year reign. God has tried mankind once more on the earth. We have seen the nation of Israel, under David the king, and the twelve apostles sitting on thrones, judging the twelve tribes of Israel with the Son of God, the King of kings, and His ruling and reigning Church, caring for the governmental processes of the world.

This age now comes to a time of testing. We have seen this time of testing allowed by God, in order that He might see the response of men, who have lived in conditions that were almost near the condition of Eden, when Adam was in the garden. We have spoken of the longevity of life on the earth; the fruitfulness of the earth; the age of a man being as the age of a tree; nations not learning war any more, beating swords into plowshares and spears into pruning hooks; of all of the nations of the world coming up to worship the Lord; of the gospel being carried into all of the Gentile nations of the world for the first time, so that every person from the least to the greatest would know the Lord; of God's blessings, through the presence of Jesus the King, on the earth during the golden age.

Now these people are to be tested. They could not be tested during the millennial age because the great archenemy of God, the devil, has been in the bottomless pit, and the Bible says a seal was set upon him, indicating that no one could ever feel his presence during the millennial age. He could not deceive the nations any more, until the thousand years be finished.

Now that the thousand years are expired, Satan is loosed out of his prison, and the Bible says, "He shall go out to deceive the nations which are in the four corners of the earth and they are called by Gog and Magog."

This is the first deception by Satan since he was cast into the bottomless pit, and chained with a chain by the angel, who came with Jesus, when He came back to earth with the resurrected saints.

Immediately, Satan is able to deceive a great multitude of people, and they come and encompass the holy city round about, but before a shot is fired, fire comes down from heaven, and the devil, with his army devoured, is cast into the lake of fire, which is the second death.

Immediately after the casting of the devil into the lake of fire and brimstone, the great White Throne judgment scene appears. The Great White Throne Judgment is different from the judgment of the living nations. It is different from the judgment of Israel. It is different from the other judgments that God has visited upon the Gentile nations, and that He has said He would visit upon the Israelite nation, up to this time.

The Scriptures make a distinction between the judgment of the nations and the judgment of the Great White Throne. In the twenty-fifth chapter of Matthew, verses 31-46, we read of the judgment of the nations, when Jesus Christ comes in great power and glory to earth, with all His holy angels, and gathers the nations of the world before Him. This judgment is on earth. Notice that the scene of the Great White Throne is *not* on earth. The judgment of the living nations judges those nations that are on the earth, following the tribulation period. The judgment of the Great White Throne judges only those wicked dead that have been in the grave from the beginning of time until the end of the thousand years. The people judged at the Great White Throne judgment are the wicked dead. The people judged in the judgment of the living nations are the living nations.

There is another difference. The judgment of the living nations, according to the context of the Bible, is *before* the millennial reign. The judgment of the Great White Throne *follows* the thousand-year reign.

Christ, the judge, is the sole judge of the judgment of the nations. God is the judge, with Christ and the Church to assist, in the judgment of the Great White Throne.

In the judgment of the nations there are two classes of people, the sheep and the goats. In the White Throne judgment, there is no direct reference to any that might be saved, but only reference to those, if any, whose name was not found written in the Lamb's Book of Life. They were all cast into the lake of fire, which is the second death.

In the sheep and goat judgment, some were destroyed and some were saved. In the Great White Throne judgment, all of them, according to the context, are cast into the lake of fire, which is the second death.

In the judgment of the living nations, there is no resurrection mentioned. In the Great White Throne judgment, there is a resurrection of all of the wicked dead of all ages.

In the judgment of the living nations, no books are opened. In the judgment of the Great White Throne, books are opened— the Book of Life and God's Book.

In the judgment of the living nations, only those generations of nations living, when Jesus comes visibly the second time, are judged. In the judgment of the Great White Throne, all generations of wicked, that have died from the beginning of time until then, are judged.

In the judgment of the living nations, only nations of men are judged. In the judgment of the Great White Throne, not only men, but angels are also judged, and in this area of judgment, the Church participates. Paul, writing to the Church at Corinth, speaking to them concerning their inability to judge among themselves the problems of the membership, says, "Know ye not that the saints will judge angels? And if we are going to judge angels, if we are going to judge the world, why can you not judge these small matters among yourselves?" (I Corinthians 6:2-4).

There is a difference in the verdicts given in judgment. In the sheep and goat judgment, some will enter into the millennial kingdom. In the Great White Throne judgment, there is no mention of anyone being saved.

In the sheep and goat judgment, there is a separation of the good from the bad. In the Great White Throne judgment, the indication is that all that are being judged are bad, and the basis of their judgment is not whether they are saved or lost, but they are judged on the basis of their deeds, and whether or not they are in the Lamb's Book of Life.

In the sheep and goat judgment, the judgment is to determine who will inhabit the earth during the millennial period, or the kingdom age. In the Great White Throne judgment, no one in the judgment scene enters into eternity and inhabits the new heaven and the new earth.

Many people, without stopping to think about the context and using good Bible logic, lump the judgment of the nations (the sheep and goat judgment) right with the judgment of the Great White Throne, and there is absolutely no similarity between them. They are not even in the same place. One is a judgment that has to do with living nations and the other is a judgment that has to do with individuals.

Following the Great White Throne judgment, there is going to be a new heaven and a new earth. Many people say, "The Bible says there is going to be a new heaven and a new earth because the Bible says that when God appeared in the Great White Throne judgment, the earth fled away." Let us examine some of these words and see really what they mean.

There are two places in the book of Revelation where it says the islands and the seas and the mountains all fled away from the face of the Lord, during the events that happened during the tribulation week, when Revelation 6-19 was fulfilled. These places did not literally flee away because they are still present in the book at the judgment seat of the Great White Throne. The earth does not flee away in the sense that it disappears. The earth is still present. In fact, the Bible teaches in the Old Testament when God created the earth, He created it to abide forever. You might have heard the saying, "That would be heaven on earth." According to Revelation 21:5, He says, "Behold I make all things new." He did not say, "Behold, I make new all things." The Greek word is *kainos* rather than *neos*. This means that the things that have to be made new are made new by the process of fire.

There are many Old Testament references that speak of the Lord shaking the earth, melting the earth with fire so that the hills and the mountains and the valleys run together, but there is no verse of Scripture that indicates that this present earth on which we live will utterly be abolished or done away with. It will be renovated. It will be made *new* (*kainos*), not in the process of making something entirely new, but in the process of making the old thing that has been cursed and degraded by man and sin pass away, and making it so new by renovation in fire that this earth will be a fit dwelling place in righteousness, for the eternal generations of men that will be upon it.

The Bible does say that there will be a new heaven *(kainos)* and a new earth *(kainos)*, and the Kosmos, made new in the sense that it is renovated, but not made new in the sense that fire destroyed it, because fire does not destroy anything. Fire only changes its state. The Bible does not teach, if you harmonize all the Scriptures concerning it, that the present heavens and earth will be completely done away with, but that they will be cleansed and purified by the use of fire, according to the desires of the Lord, as He purges it and makes it a fit place for the residence of His people.

Let us use a little logic. Why would the Lord remove the curse from the earth? Why would the Lord give all of the animal creation new natures? Remember—the lion lies down with the lamb. The lion and the carnivorous beasts, their internal systems having been changed to where they eat grass like the ox, rather than meat, and of the enmity between man and beast done away with? Why would He do all of this in order just to burn it up completely?

There is every reason to believe that, when the fire from heaven comes down to destroy the devil and his angels as they encamp about the camp of the saints, the camp of the saints is spared. In the Bible, we know that there is a fire that burns material things and does not burn people—because of God's intervention.

Do you remember the story of the three Hebrew children? The furnace was heated seven times hotter than it had ever been heated before and all of the elements that they threw into the furnace were burned up by the natural fire, but the son of God, or the presence of the messenger of God, in the flames was with the children of Israel and prevented them from being burned up. This was protection by God!

Nevertheless, the earth being renovated by fire, and the elements of the earth (*elements* does not necessarily mean from the language, the oxygen, the hydrogen and all of these things we call elements today—but it does mean the elements of sin, disease, sickness, degradation, pollution and all of these things that cause the misery of mankind) will be burned up, because they will have no place in the renewed heavens and the new earth.

Following the renewal—the Bible says, "And I, John, saw the holy city, New Jerusalem, coming down from God out of heaven."

Where is it coming to? It is coming down to earth. "And I heard a great voice out of heaven saying, behold, the tabernacle of God is with men." He is speaking about the people who are to inherit the new heavens and the new earth. We have already been told what has happened to the Church. Members of the Church have become spirit beings. They are in body and spirit like the Son of God. They are made like Him. John said, "We shall see Him as He is. As He is, we shall be."

They have ruled and reigned, as spirit beings with the Lord, during the kingdom age. They will be ruling and reigning, with God and Christ and the other angels and spirit beings, in the new heavens and new earth, but there must be someone over whom they will rule and reign. They are not just going to rule and reign over empty space. These people John sees, who believed on Jesus, and who dwelt in righteousness during the millennial age, and were spared the fire that fell from heaven on God and Magog, and who are preserved during the renovation of the earth, will dwell in happiness on the new earth.

The Bible says, "The tabernacle of God is with men," so the tabernacle of God must be on the new earth. God will dwell with them and they shall be His people, and God Himself shall be with them, and be their God. He will be so intimate with them that He shall wipe away all tears from their eyes. There will be no more death, for death and hell were destroyed when Jesus delivered up the kingdom to the Father. There will be no more death from this time on, because death is destroyed. It will have no effect on the new earth whatsoever.

Former things are passed away and behold all things are become new. He says, "He that overcometh shall inherit all things and I will be his God and he shall be my son." Immediately in that context we read in the next verse, as we have read concerning the dwelling of God with His people on the earth, "But the fearful, and unbelieving, and the abominable, and murderers, and whoremongers, and sorcerers, and idolators, and all liars, shall have their part in the lake which burneth with fire and brimstone: which is the second death."

This simply indicates that none of those people, who lived in this manner of fleshly living, will be able to be a part of God's heaven and God's earth and God's new people, and if you want to find about where these people are, and the fact that they will be able to be observed during the reign of God eternally, on the new earth and the new heavens, turn to the last verse of the last chapter of the book of Isaiah and see what you discover.

I want to speak to you now about the bride, the Lamb's wife, the holy city, the New Jerusalem, and what it means in the Bible. The city is not a cube, but according to the Bible, the city is a series of elevated places, or mountains, beginning with one from 250 feet high in the inside circumference of the wall, and extending to the height of 1500 miles in the center. This particular area which is called the New Jerusalem, is 1500 miles by 1500 miles all the way around and the height of the city is 1500 miles. From the height of the 1500 miles, John could see the whole city. Picture that in your mind. The angel took him to the top of the highest mountain in the city, and he could see all around. He could see streets, rivers, trees, people, and he could see all of these things because the angel allowed him to see it. In the Bible, it is called Mount Zion, the mount of the congregation in the sides of the north, the mountain of His holiness, the holy city, the New Jerusalem, and it has been in preparation from since the time that men on earth began to look for it, way back in the early ages of the beginning of mankind.

The Bible tells us of its measurements, its materials, its age, its streets, etc., but we go on to the twenty-second verse of the twenty-first chapter of Revelation.

Actually, on the mount in the highest mountain, there will be a literal temple, but what John has been referring to here is that, since God has tabernacled with men, there will be no need for men to go up as they did in times past to a building in order to worship God, because men will meet with God all of the time in the heavenly kingdom—that is, in the new heavens and the new earth.

The city has no need of the sun. Many think that when the end of the age comes the sun and the moon will no longer shine. They think this because in the book of Revelation, the revelator says that the moon turns to blood and the sun turns dark as sackcloth. We read again where parts of the sun will be darkened. The entire context of Scriptures about the sun, moon, and the earth indicates to those who make the study that God has said, "As long as my word abides, the sun, moon, the earth and the stars will remain."

God did not create this universe just to burn it up at the end of the life of mankind in the present age on the earth. The *city* has no need of the sun because God is there, and the Lamb is there, "for the glory of God did lighten it and the Lamb is the light thereof."

The Scriptures say, "And the nations of them which are saved . . ." Where are nations to be? On the new earth. "The nations of them that are saved shall walk in the light of this city: and the kings of the earth do bring their glory and honor into it. And the gates of it shall not be shut at all by day: for there shall be no night there." In fact, the gates will never be shut.

Continually, throughout eternity, the perpetual nations of men living on the earth will bring the honor and glory of the kings into this city of heaven where God, Christ, the angels, the sons of God (the raptured Church), will be ruling and reigning for all eternity, over all of God's creation in all of the universe forever!

"And there shall in no wise enter into it any thing that defileth, neither whatsoever worketh abomination, or maketh a lie, but they which are written in the Lamb's book of life." This means that all who do these things have been taken care of by casting them into the lake of fire, which is the second death, before the New Heavens and the New earth appear, for the eternal generations of man to live on.

John says, "And he showed me a pure river of water of life." If this is not a real world that we are talking about, there is no need to have a river there. The reason there is the river of the water of life and the tree of life, which is referred to in the first and second verses of Revelation 22, is that the people who believed and obeyed Jesus in the millennial age, and who will make up the generations of people in the new earth, are not classified as spirit beings, as the Church that was raptured prior to the millennial age. The Church will be immortal because of having been translated and changed in a moment, in the twinkling of an eye. The Church will have put on the same spiritual body that Jesus has. Faithful and devout members of the body of Christ will never need to drink of the water of life, and eat of the tree of life, because eternal life was given to them when they accepted Christ in the Church Age. The eternal generations of men who live on the new earth from the millennial age must have the water of life and the tree of life, in order that their lives may continue.

The Scriptures say, "And the leaves of the tree were for the healing of the nations. And there shall be no more curse: but the throne of God and of the Lamb shall be in it; and his servants shall serve him." The faithful angels, the redeemed men from the Gentile nations of the world, those men and women called out by the preaching of the gospel of Christ, and all others who have not rebelled against the rule and reign of God and Christ in all of the ages are these servants of God and they will serve Him in that day.

"And there shall be no night there." Again, it is referring to the city, New Jerusalem. "And they need no candle, neither light of the sun; for the Lord God giveth them light and they shall reign forever and ever." This has reference to the servants who shall have the name of God in their foreheads.

He said:

These things are faithful and true, and the Lord God of the holy prophets sent his angel to show unto his servants the things which must shortly be done. Behold, I come quickly: blessed is he that keepeth the sayings of this book. And I, John, saw these things and heard them. And when I had heard and seen, I fell down to worship before the feet of the angel which showed me these things. Then saith he unto me, See thou do it not: for I am thy fellow servant, and of thy brethren the prophets, and of them which keep the sayings of this book: worship God. And he saith unto me, Seal not the sayings of the prophecy of this book; for the time is at hand. (Revelation 22:6-10)

Let those who claim that you cannot literally interpret the book of Revelation and the prophecy of Daniel, and the prophecies that Jesus made, note that, in Revelation 22:10, the angel says, "Don't seal up the sayings of this book." Wherever the words "do not seal up" are used in Scripture, it indicates that the prophecy is to be read and understood by everybody, and this is why there is a blessing attached to those who will keep these truths, which are not hidden truths, but which are plain, simple, literal truths, written for men in plain, simple language to be understood. If men refuse to believe them, of course, the truth is hidden from them. It is just that simple. When men refuse to believe them, the truth is sealed, not by the angel or by John, but by their own unbelief.

The eternal state of men is to be as they are, when they stop living on earth. All through the Scripture, from Adam to Revelation, it teaches that if a man dies filthy, that is the way he will be for eternity. If a man dies righteous, that is the way he will be eternally. If a man dies guilty of gross immorality and sin, that is the way he will be eternally. As a tree falls, so shall it lie.

This is why it is important, in any age, to know the revealed will of God and to do it, because if death, or if the Lord comes, or if we are snatched out into eternity, the very condition that we are in when we die is the condition in which we shall be eternally:

He that is unjust, let him be unjust still. He that is holy let him be holy still. Behold, I come quickly and my reward is with me, to give to every man according as his work shall be. Blessed are they that do his commandments, that they may have the right to the tree of life. (Revelation 22:2) *12*

There are two rights for the people who have loved the Lord and followed Him. This does not refer to the raptured Church, but to the natural people who were saved during the millennial reign and who did not participate in the rebellion of the devil at the end of the millennial age. These have two rights—first of all, the right to the tree of life. Why do they have the tree of life? If *they* are sons of God and they are already immortal, why do they have the tree of life? The tree of life will not be for the raptured Church, in the sense that it was for Adam, in the early garden of Eden. The tree of life will be for those people who are like Adam— the natural generations of righteous men who will live forever, and the thing that enables them to live forever is the right to the tree of life, and the right to enter the New Jerusalem. Why would they have to have the right to enter the New Jerusalem in order to live forever? What is there? It is the only place they will find the tree of life. If they do not have that right, they will not live forever. Everyone from the millennial age who makes it to that time referred to in Revelation 22 will automatically have the right to the tree of life, and the right to enter the New Jerusalem.

Jesus says, as He affirms the authenticity of the book: "I, Jesus, have sent mine angel to testify these times unto you in the churches. I am the root and the offspring of David." This was prophesied by Gabriel to Mary, when Jesus was born. He said, "You shall conceive in your womb and bring forth a child. You shall call his name Jesus. He shall reign on the throne of his father David and rule over the kingdom of Israel forever." I believe that, and Jesus confirms it in the end of the book. He says, "I am the root and the offspring of David, and the bright and morning star. And the Spirit and the bride say, Come."

The bride of Christ has often been said to be the Church. That is partly true, but in the Holy City that shall come will be the redeemed saints of all of the ages, who were caught up with the Church, in the resurrection of the righteous dead, and the tribulation martyrs, who were caught up before the end of the tribulation week. They all looked for a city whose ruler and maker is God, which is to come. We look for a city, and so, scripturally, the bride of Christ is not a New Testament bride only, but it is the faithful believers in the will of God from any age who will inhabit the city of God with Christ, and who will rule and reign over the natural generations of nations on earth, for an eternity. So the bride of Christ is not only the people, but it is also the city. It is a conglomerate —it is everything in one. All of the resurrected saints, as well as the city, that has been prepared for them, even as Jesus said it would be.

The great invitation of God to all of the perpetual living generations of men in the New Earth will be, "Come and take the water of life and eat of the tree of life and live forever under the wonderful blessings of Almighty God."

In the sixteenth chapter of Revelation, the seventeenth verse, God said, "It is done." Here are some of the things that are "done," that make up this place that we call heaven—the place that we have dreamed and thought about, and never had a clear picture of. "It is done." The sinful career of the immediate heavens and earth is ended. That which began was ended, once and for all, and will never again be able to curse and harass mankind. The renovation of the heavens and the earth —"all things made new"—is completed. All that needed to be made new are now a fit dwelling place for God, and for the people who have been redeemed. All rebels are put down. The Scriptures say that Jesus must rule until all things are brought under His power, and, when the devil and his armies are finally crushed at the end of the thousand years, and death has been put in the lake of fire, all things *then* are put under His feet, and He will deliver the kingdom up to God. The earth is turned back to God. In the third chapter of Acts, the apostle Peter speaks of the times of the restoration of all things (Acts 3:19-22). He is speaking of the times of refreshing that will come when all things will be restored to the state of innocence and purity that existed in the beginning. All the rebels that have ever lived from the time of Adam are judged and confined to the lake of fire where they will be eternally.

God will be recognized as the supreme ruler of the universe. He will be ruling with Christ and with the Church under Him. This is the promise. If the Church of the Lord Jesus Christ realized her part in God's scheme of redemption for the earth; if she realized that the purpose of the gospel is to take from the nations of natural men a spiritual people, who will reign and rule with Jesus, she would not need another attendance campaign, nor would she be begging and pleading with people to come and accept the gospel. God's original plan for man in the universe will be realized. Men will be able to live and fulfill the plan that God had for Adam in the beginning, when all of these blessings we have spoken of come to the renewed Heavens and Earth.

God's form of government and His own righteous being will be vindicated. He will have given man every chance. No man, since he will be judged according to his own deeds, and his own opportunities, will have a chance to say, "God, you weren't fair to me." In fact, the last Great White Throne Judgment will be the most severe of them all because many men will be just as foolish in the millennial age as Mother Eve was, and say, "Maybe we can do it better ourselves." They will try to take over control of earth once more.

God's throne and God's headquarters will be moved from the third heavens, to which Paul said he was caught up and saw things that were not lawful for a man to speak of, and will be established on the New Earth. He will walk, talk, and dwell with men. The Scriptures teach this. I hope you believe it.

Even so, come Lord Jesus (Revelation 22:20).